The Personality Factor

Dianne Langley

The Rural Publishing Company

First published by The Rural Publishing Company 2025.

Copyright © Dianne Langley 2025

Print (Paperback): 978-1-923008-30-4
eBook: 978-1-923008-31-1

This work is copyright. Apart from any use permitted under the Copyright Act 1968, no part of this publication may be reproduced, stored in a retrieval system or transmitted in any form or by any means, electronic, mechanical, photocopying, recording or otherwise, without the prior written permission of Dianne Langley or The Rural Publishing Company.

Cover Design: The Rural Publishing Company
Typesetting & Design: The Rural Publishing Company

The Rural Publishing Company
Website: https://theruralpublishingcompany.com.au
Email: hello@theruralpublishingcompany.com.au

Contents

Introduction	1
1. What is the Personality Factor?	9
2. The Personality Factor and Parenting	53
3. The Personality Factor and Teaching	77
4. The Personality Factor and Mental Health	105
Conclusion	123
Useful Resources	129
About the Author	137

Introduction

I HAVE TURNED SEVENTY and I still don't know what I want to be when I grow up! I found myself as lost and unprepared for the next chapter in my life as I did when I left high school over fifty years ago. The seventy-year milestone really has been a time of reflection; a time of reconciling my life and a time of mulling over what lies ahead. There have been many accomplishments that I have been proud of over that time, but one thing has been constant since my mid-thirties. You could say that since then my life's work has encompassed the rich theory of Jung's Personality Types using the MBTI® (Myers-Briggs Type Indicator)*. I have used it in many settings, the most important of which was using it to bring up my children in the best way I could. I also have used it in teaching, counselling, and training courses.

It has been clear to me that not enough attention is paid to personality – I call it the Personality Factor – and how it can play a vital role in the way we manage our lives. Over thirty years ago I wanted to write a book to share the insights I'd gained from knowing about my Personality Factor, but it has taken me a lifetime of experiences to get here. Now, I feel that it is a waste of my life's work if I do not document my experiences to pass on to the next generations.

Have you ever wondered why you don't seem to fit in, and nobody seems to understand you?

Do you wish that your relationships with significant others could be better?

Do you ever feel guilty that you just don't seem to get along with your child?

Do you wonder why some of your students don't seem to 'get it'?

Do you worry about your child's progress at school?

Have you worked with colleagues who seem to make your life unbearable?

If some of the above resonates for you, then this book is a 'must read'.

The Personality Factor is an anecdotal account of aspects of my parenting and working life. It highlights the importance that an awareness of personality played in negotiating around hurdles presented to me along the way. It also provides a look at the theory of Personality Types by Carl Jung written in the 1920's. My aim is to create an awareness of the importance of considering the Personality Factor, using the knowledge and experience I have accumulated over the last thirty years or so.

In typical fashion of my own Personality Factor, I want the world to live in harmony; for everyone to get on with each other. I want everybody to reach their full potential. I acknowledge that each person will take away something different after reading this book. However, if I can help even a few people make more sense of their lives and become better versions of themselves, then my work is done!

This book may not have all the answers, but it can provide a way to look at things differently and to change what can be changed by being mindful of your Personality Factor. Knowing my own Personality Factor has been the single most helpful tool for me in my life.

While there are many resources available to learn about personality, I believe one of the simplest ways to find out your Personality Factor is to undertake the Myers-Briggs Type Indicator (MBTI®). The MBTI® was developed by Isabell Myers and Katherine Briggs in 1962 to more easily access the theory of *Personality Types* written by Carl Jung in 1921.

I was first introduced to Personality Type in the late 1980's. I loved it so much I undertook my MBTI® Accreditation in 1988 and have continued using it ever since. I completed a more in-depth training course in MBTI® in 1992 and undertook MBTI® STEP II accredited training in 2015. It has been an invaluable tool for me to understand my place in the world. Most importantly, it has enabled me to better understand other people in my life, my parents, my siblings, my partners, my children and my work colleagues.

There is a wealth of valuable resources on personality already available, so rather than writing another textbook, I want to provide a book that is easy to read and enlightening at the same time. The purpose is to create an anecdotal account for the uninitiated, about how knowledge and understanding of your Personality Factor can have a significant bearing on understanding yourself better and appreciating other people while managing your life. I want it to be available more widely to the everyday reader rather than only the practitioners of Personality Type Theory. My greatest challenge is being able to share my passion and knowledge in a way you will understand.

This book, nevertheless, may become a stepping stone for you to become aware of your own Personality Factor and its importance in helping you navigate through life. I urge everyone to have the courage to gain an understanding of their Personality Factor, to give yourself permission to be yourself and appreciate the differences in other people.

The first book I read about personality was *Please Understand Me* by David Keirsey and Marilyn Bates. I believe David was inspired in part by Henry David Thoreau's 1854 work, *Walden* where Thoreau says, 'If a man does not keep pace with his companions, perhaps it is because he hears a different drummer. Let him step to the music which he hears, however measured or far away.' The first page of Keirsey's book really struck a chord with me when my marriage counsellor first introduced it to me way back in the mid 1980's. Until then I really thought that everybody wanted the same things as I did. It was a poignant moment when I realised that was not the case. It has led me to write this book. Perhaps it will be the beginning of your journey with your Personality Factor.

The following is an updated version of the extract from that page.

Different Drums and Different Drummers

If you do not want what I want, please try not to tell me that my want is wrong.

Or if my beliefs are different from yours, at least pause before you set out to correct them.

Or if my emotion seems less or more intense than yours, given the same circumstances, try not to ask me to feel other than I do.

Or if I act, or fail to act, in the manner of your design for action, please let me be.

I do not for the moment at least, ask you to understand me. That will come only when you are willing to give up trying to change me into a copy of you.

If you will allow me any of my own wants, or emotions, or beliefs, or actions, then you open yourself to the possibility that someday these ways of mine might not seem so wrong and might finally appear as right - for me. To put up with me is the first step to understanding me.

Not that you embrace my ways as right for you, but that you are no longer irritated or disappointed with me for my seeming waywardness.

And one day, perhaps, in trying to understand me, you might come to prize my differences, and, far from seeking to change me, might preserve and even cherish those differences.

I may be your spouse, your parent, your offspring, your friend, your colleague. But whatever our relation, this I know: You and I are fundamentally different and both of us have to march to our own drummer.

From *Please Understand Me II* by David Keirsey & Marilyn Bates

* *Myers-Briggs Type Indicator, Myers Briggs, MBTI, the MBTI logo, Step I, Step II, Step III and Introduction to Type are trademarks or registered trademarks of Myers & Briggs Foundation in the United States and other countries.*

Chapter One

What is the Personality Factor?

I USE THE TERM 'Personality Factor' as a way of describing that part of us which is often overlooked when managing life's challenges and obligations. The Personality Factor, as referred to in the Introduction refers to the unique talents and strengths we are born with, the things that make us different from each other. Our Personality Factor affects all aspects of our lives and can play a significant role in understanding and managing our world.

While I started my working life as a teacher, there were times when I worked in areas other than teaching. Besides assisting students and teachers and parents, I used my knowledge and expertise with the Personality Factor to help many people from all walks of life to allow them to know themselves better and to support them to make positive changes in their lives.

I found that the Personality Factor was well received by everyone I introduced it to. They found the insights gained from knowing their Personality Factor, to be extremely useful to better understand themselves. It offered insights into how to manage the situation they were in at the time of my involvement. Sometimes I received immediate feedback especially if I had conducted a group workshop. Mostly however, I really didn't know whether my intervention with the Personality Factor was appreciated or not. Significant occasions which cemented my belief that the Personality Factor had indeed helped other people as much as it had helped me, were when people who I had worked with came up to me on the street sometime later and thanked me for providing them with the knowledge and understanding they had gained.

The people I have helped most over the past thirty years in my roles as teacher and counsellor, were people who weren't in tune with their Personality Factor or who thought that they didn't fit in and felt that nobody understood them. I can personally relate to this as I really didn't know myself as a young adult and have often felt misunderstood throughout my life. The knowledge and insights I gained from knowing my Personality Factor have been powerful and very useful in helping me know who I am. I now accept that not everyone sees things the same way I do, and that their way of seeing the world is as valid for them as my way is for me. Finding out that my personality type makes up only about 1% of the population went a long way towards explaining why I didn't seem to fit in much of the time. If only I'd known my Personality Factor in my formative years! While I don't regret the things I've done in my life, even a rudimentary knowledge of my Personality Factor would have helped me navigate my way through my teenage and young adult years with much less angst. Unfortunately, this information wasn't available to me then. Nevertheless, I am truly grateful to have discovered it when I did and feel privileged to be able to share this information now.

Some background:

In the mid 1980's, I was having serious marriage problems. My husband couldn't see any logical reason that I should participate in creative pursuits given my workload managing the household. It was important for him to have a tidy house. I, on the other hand, needed to do something to keep me from going 'crazy' trying to keep up with the housework especially after the children arrived. I couldn't comprehend why he didn't seem to appreciate how hard it was for me to keep the house shipshape while looking after three young children. Organising my external environment was not something that I was particularly good at. I also felt that it was more important to play with my children than to have the clothes folded neatly. This is clearly something that my husband and I didn't agree on. While there are many factors that may result in a marriage breakdown, for me, I now understand it was my Personality Factor and that of my husband's which contributed significantly to the lack of effective communication in our marriage and our failure to resolve our issues. I believe that it is extremely important to go to counselling. Yet it has been widely documented that people with my ex-husband's Personality Factor are less likely to seek counselling. So it was that I went to counselling by myself. I am pleased that I did and so thankful that my marriage counsellor had knowledge of the MBTI®.

When my marriage counsellor asked me to do a personality assessment and suggested I read the book '*Please Understand Me*', it was the beginning of my understanding of my own Personality Factor. I was astounded at the insightfulness and usefulness of the information. I gleaned a better understanding of myself and the other people in my life, especially my children. My counsellor was impressed with the insights I had gained about my children and said to me, 'Wouldn't it be great if parents could have this knowledge about their children?' With my background in teaching, it was then that I decided I wanted to share this knowledge with other parents and teachers. Thus, it became my life's passion to do just that.

It also helped me understand the differences between my husband and me, however, it takes two people in a marriage to want to continue in the relationship; so, we went our separate ways. My knowledge of my Personality Factor helped me to understand that some expectations I had of my partner were unrealistic. It was not that he was a 'bad person' – it was simply that he had different inherent values and core needs than I did and without an acceptance and understanding of each other's differences, no common ground could be found. It also allowed me to remove the 'blame' often associated with failed marriages.

While I believe there can be no liking without likeness, there is no right or wrong when it comes to relationships. When we are talking about relationships, whether it's romantic, friends or work colleagues, most can endure some difficulties and trauma. However, there is often no coming back from unmet or unrealistic expectations that can't be managed through acceptance and effective communication. How often are we attracted to someone who is different to us and admire those differences only to eventually say 'I like you but why aren't you more like me?'. How often do we have friends or even work colleagues who may seem to rub us up the wrong way? These differences can easily become a source of distress when people don't understand that sometimes the expectations they may have of each other, could be idealistic and perhaps unrealistic. I know that even a basic understanding of the Personality Factor may circumvent misunderstandings in relationships of all kinds. It can also promote a level of acceptance of each other even though each one may be fundamentally different in nature.

While you can't change other people, this knowledge could help to change the way you manage your own journey. You might see things differently and accept that others around you who may potentially cause you conflict are not necessarily bad. They are merely different to you and innately want different things.

A knowledge of our Personality Factor has many applications in how we live our lives.

For example:

- Properly used, it can be an extremely useful tool in gaining an understanding of ourselves and others.

- We can understand what things energise us and what things deplete our reserves.

- This knowledge may help raise our self-esteem and increase our personal effectiveness, and it could possibly become a major player in breaking the cycle of past negatives.

- It could lessen some frustrations in communication for ourselves with family, relationships and work colleagues.

- Children's behavioural problems at home and at school may be better understood and better managed, helping them to become happy, effective human beings.

What is your Personality Factor?

You could be an individual, a parent, a partner, a friend, a student, a worker. I believe that knowing your Personality Factor is key to developing better relationships with yourself and others around you.

In my workshops and counselling sessions, I use the following exercise to introduce people to the concept of recognising their inherent talents and the importance of using them effectively.

If you have a piece of paper and a pen/pencil handy, you can do this exercise:

First, take a pen/pencil in your *preferred* hand and write your name. Think about how it felt during the process.

Next take a pen/pencil in your *least preferred* hand and write your name. Now think about how it felt during this process.

I find that most people generally report that when they write their name using their preferred hand, the process is easy, it comes naturally, and the results are good – mostly neat and tidy.

They go on to report that when they use their least preferred hand, while they can do it, it takes more effort and concentration. It is awkward, they are slower, and the results are not as good – mostly childlike, untidy writing.

It has nothing to do with which hand you write with; the analogy lies in seeing that your innate gifts and talents come naturally and easily, and the results are good. I'm sure you have noticed that other people can do some things more easily than you can, while you are naturally better at some things than others.

Carl Jung, through his research, proposed that people are different in fundamental ways. They want different things, and they believe different things. No amount of trying is going to change them and to understand other people, we must first know ourselves.

The MBTI® is a non-threatening questionnaire where you decide how accurate the result is. It cannot determine specific skills or level of competency in skills. It can show some of your core preferences, tendencies and characteristics. Its usefulness may depend on it being interpreted by a qualified MBTI® practitioner. When used correctly it may help people who live or work together to understand how previously irritating, and seemingly obstructive, differences might become a source of amusement, interest and strength.

It is impossible for me to describe differences and behaviours of your Personality Factor without referring to MBTI® terminology according to Carl Jung, so I will provide a brief description of Jung's Theory of Personality Types. This may be the beginning of your journey in considering your Personality Factor when gathering information and making decisions. The insights gleaned may well take out some of the guesswork, especially when dealing with problems which don't seem to have an obvious answer or have solutions that work for some people and not for others.

Jung's Theory of Personality Types and the Myers-Briggs Type Indicator (MBTI®) explained

The MBTI® is not a party game. It is based on Carl Jung's Theory of Personality Types and it has more than fifty years of research and development behind it. This Indicator has been widely used for decades to understand normal personality differences. It is used to better understand ourselves, our motivations, our strengths and potential areas for growth. It also helps to better understand and appreciate those who differ from us.

The Myers-Briggs Type Indicator provides you with a four-letter 'Type' based on how the questionnaire is answered. It consists of a choice from each of the four preference scales of Jung's theory, reported in the MBTI®. In your exploration of type theory, you are the one who ultimately decides which type description fits you best, and which type is your true type. Your true type represents your natural preferences.

Remember no preference or type is considered better or worse than another. There is no 'right' or 'wrong' Personality Factor.

Preference Scale 1

What is the direction and focus of your personal energy?

E or **I**? **E** is for **E**xtraversion, and **I** is for **I**ntroversion.

E	OR	**I**
You prefer to focus on the outer world of people and things.		You prefer to focus on the inner world of thoughts and reflections.

An **E**xtravert's fundamental stimulation is from the environment. An **I**ntrovert's essential stimulation is from within.

We all use both but *prefer* either **E**xtraversion or **I**ntroversion.

Preference Scale 2

How do you prefer to gather information?

S or **N**? **S** is for **S**ensing, and **N** is for i**N**tuition. (Please note that because **I** is used for preference scale 1, the letter **N** is used for i**N**tuition.)

The **S**ensing function takes in information by way of the five senses – sight, sound, touch, taste, and smell. The i**N**tuiting function processes information by way of a 'sixth sense' or hunch.

> **S**
> You tend to focus on the present and on concrete information gained from your senses.

OR

> **N**
> You prefer to focus on the inner world of ideas and impressions.

Both ways of perceiving and taking in information are used by everyone but we have a *preference* for **S**ensing or i**N**tuition.

Preference Scale 3

How do you prefer to make decisions?

T or **F**? **T** is for **T**hinking, and **F** is for **F**eeling.

With the **T**hinking function decisions are made based on logic and objective considerations. With the **F**eeling function, decisions are based on personal, subjective values.

> **T**
> You tend to base your decisions on logic and on objective analysis of cause and effect.

OR

> **F**
> You tend to base your decisions primarily on subjective evaluation of person-centred concerns.

Both ways of deciding and evaluating are used by everyone, but we *prefer* **T**hinking or **F**eeling.

Preference Scale 4

How do you deal with the outer world?

J or **P**? **J** is for **J**udging, and **P** is for **P**erceiving.

A **J**udging lifestyle is decisive, planned and orderly. A **P**erceiving lifestyle is adaptable and spontaneous.

> **J**
> You like a planned and organised approach to life and prefer to have things settled.

OR

> **P**
> You like a flexible and spontaneous approach to life and prefer to keep your options open.

Both attitudes are part of everyone's lifestyle, but we *prefer* **Judging** or **Perceiving**.

The combinations of the eight preferences in the MBTI® model produce sixteen personality types.

These are:

ISTJ – ISFJ – ISTP – ISFP – ESTP – ESFP – ESTJ – ESFJ INFJ – INTJ – INFP – INTP – ENFP – ENTP – ENFJ – ENTJ

Remember though, that The Personality Factor is more than simply knowing the four basic preferences **E** or **I**, **S** or **N**, **T** or

F, **J** or **P**. An understanding of how the four functions relate to each other, and in what order you prefer to use them, can tell you a great deal about yourself. It can determine how you prefer to communicate, what you consider to be important, and the kinds of activities and careers you may find motivating or stressful. The functions develop by being used consciously and purposefully for things that matter.

Using our preferred function is like using our preferred hand. If we are using our least preferred function, it's like using our other hand. It is important to identify our strengths and use them. Stress may come from constantly having to use our least favoured preferences more than we use our preferred function.

Then again answer this. How effective are we if we only use our preferred hand? Imagine if our other hand was not available and we could only use our preferred hand to do things throughout the day. Most people will say that they are not effective at all. We need our other hand to help get dressed, tie shoelaces, carry heavy items to name a few. These activities all need both hands. However, when it comes down to tasks that require one hand, our preferred hand is most often used.

It is the same with our personality preferences. We need to use both to be truly effective. The important thing is to be the real you, using your own unique gifts as much as possible. We need to use our least preferred functions to provide balance; but then life may become very exhausting if we are frequently engaging in tasks requiring activities which do not reflect our natural talents. Of course, we can still do all things and it's important that we do. But remember, only do the challenging things in moderation. This way we will maintain effectiveness and avoid the stress which comes from constantly doing things that do not come naturally. It is important to recognise our strengths and use them. It is also important to avoid constantly being something we are not by always having to use our least preferred functions excessively.

For example, my preference is for Introversion. While this doesn't automatically mean that I am shy, it does explain why constantly being around lots of people for a long period of time can be draining for me. Understanding this means that I can spend some time by myself to recharge my batteries without feeling guilty. I know that this is important for me; it doesn't necessarily mean that I am being anti-social.

Characteristics of the 16 personality types:

SENSING		INTUITION	
ISTJ Trustee, Steward I Depth of concentration S Reliance on facts T Logic and analysis J Organisation	**ISFJ** Preserver, Server I Depth of concentration S Reliance on facts F Warmth and sympathy J Organisation	**INFJ** Author, Seer I Depth of concentration N Grasp of possibilities F Warmth and sympathy J Organisation	**INTJ** Theoretician, Academician I Depth of concentration N Grasp of possibilities T Logic and analysis J Organisation
ISTP Artisan, Guard I Depth of concentration S Reliance on facts T Logic and analysis P Adaptability	**ISFP** Artist, Appreciator I Depth of concentration S Reliance on facts F Warmth and sympathy P Adaptability	**INFP** Seeker, Searcher I Depth of concentration N Grasp of possibilities F Warmth and sympathy P Adaptability	**INTP** Architect, Philosopher I Depth of concentration N Grasp of possibilities T Logic and analysis P Adaptability
ESTP Promoter, Trouble Shooter E Breadth of Interests S Reliance on facts T Logic and analysis P Adaptability	**ESFP** Entertainer, Reveller E Breadth of Interests S Reliance on facts F Warmth and sympathy P Adaptability	**ENFP** Celebrater, Enthusiast E Breadth of Interests N Grasp of possibilities F Warmth and sympathy P Adaptability	**ENTP** Debater, Inventor E Breadth of Interests N Grasp of possibilities T Logic and analysis P Adaptability
ESTJ Administrator, Organiser E Breadth of Interests S Reliance on facts T Logic and analysis J Organisation	**ESFJ** Provider, Salesperson E Breadth of Interests S Reliance on facts F Warmth and sympathy J Organisation	**ENFJ** Entrepreneur, Ringmaster E Breadth of Interests N Grasp of possibilities F Warmth and sympathy J Organisation	**ENTJ** Strategist, Commander E Breadth of Interests N Grasp of possibilities T Logic and analysis J Organisation

Please remember there is no right or wrong Type. Our own Personality Factor is the right one – for us. The percentages quoted in the following table may not be precisely reported. It does, however, show that all types are not equal in terms of representation in the population.

Distribution of the 16 personality types:

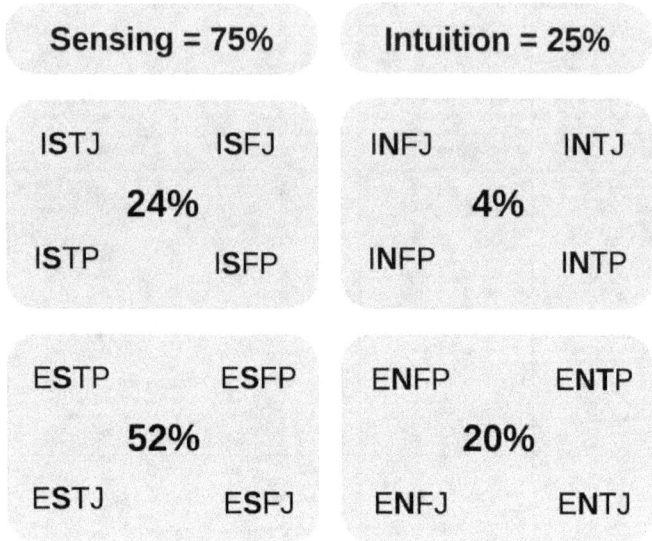

Please Note: The percentages written here may not be totally accurate at the time of printing.

Have you ever wondered why some people we know seem to be on the same wavelength while others drive us crazy? From the table, we can see that the people whose Personality Factor includes the **S** – Sensing function make up roughly **75%** of the population while only **25%** prefer the **N** – i**N**tuition function.

It is interesting to me that people with **E** – Extravert and **S** – Sensing, make up over 50% of the population. When four Types out of sixteen (**ES**TP, **ES**FP, **ES**TJ and **ES**FJ – see table above), make up more than half the population, it can explain why some others may seem to doubt themselves. In my experience, I have found that people from this group seem to fit in and could relate to most others more easily. However, they would often be puzzled by others around them who were not like them.

In my work over the past thirty years or so, it was usually the people who were least represented in the population who came to me for help to understand why they didn't see things the same way as their family, peers, partners, and the like. Finding out their Personality Factor was crucial in understanding the dynamics causing some of the problems they were having. I also found that just over fifty percent of those people who did the MBTI® with me, initially reported results other than their true type. It wasn't until further investigation was undertaken, that their true Type was discovered. Incorrect Type can be reported for many reasons. It may well be the way we answer the questions according to the 'mood' we are in, or whether we answer how we think we should be rather than who we really are. Perhaps, it relates to the stage of life we are in. Remember, you decide how accurate the report is for you. Sometimes, the reason the MBTI® results are put into a drawer and forgotten is because the Type reported didn't resonate and no further investigation was sought.

For this reason, even though I have provided an overview of Myers-Briggs Type Indicator®, it is essential that professional help is sought from a qualified MBTI® practitioner to fully understand your Personality Factor.

Knowing my Personality Factor has provided me with an entirely new level of understanding of myself and my place in the world. It explained why, in my late teens to early adulthood, I always seemed to feel uncomfortable at parties or other large gatherings. I didn't see the need for small talk and had trouble joining in a conversation with a large group of people. Because I didn't know my Personality Factor at that time, I felt like I didn't fit in and that there must be something wrong with me. What a revelation it has been to find out that my reaction to parties was a perfectly normal reaction for a person with a preference for **Introversion**. After learning about the **Introversion/Extraversion** dynamics, I discovered ways to best serve my need for **Introversion** while still building strong relationships.

With Extraverts, what you see is what you get. They put their best foot forward. You usually know how an Extravert is thinking or feeling. With Introverts on the other hand, they live in their inner world and tend to keep their thoughts and feelings to themselves. This means that their best is less visible. They will often only show their best when they get to know you or are comfortable with the situation.

Extraversion

- Freely expressed emotions and thoughts.
- Often quick to get to know.
- Friendly and talkative.
- Often acts first and then (maybe) reflects.

Introversion

- Keeps emotions and thoughts private.
- Often reserved and quiet so may take time to get to know.
- Usually reflects first and then (maybe) act.

As one who prefers Introversion, I must search within to find the answer to provide the response I am happy with. There have been many times where it has taken me too long to offer up what I really wanted to say, so I have missed the opportunity to be heard. I have realised that when pressed, the thing which comes off the top of head isn't necessarily what I really want to say. My strategy became – if it really didn't matter, I'd let my initial comments go through to the keeper; if it was important, I'd bring up the conversation again where possible and put forth my real view.

With a preference for Introversion, it was incredibly difficult for me to get my much-needed time alone while working full time and bringing up three children. I discovered that if I sat down to watch TV at home, I usually wasn't interrupted much. So that became my 'alone time'. While it looked like I was 'doing something' – watching TV, I was simply 'zoning out' preserving my equilibrium. If you asked me about the TV show, I couldn't tell you much. I also learned to tell my children – 'let me think about it and I'll get back to you,' when they asked me about something important. This meant that I didn't feel pressured into giving an inappropriate answer. Later I said what I wanted to say. This was often not the case before I knew about my Personality Factor, causing many disagreements. I could also use this strategy with my Extravert friends who expected an immediate answer and thought that my silence, (I was thinking about my answer), meant I didn't want to participate in the conversation, especially if it was a phone conversation where nothing was being said and there were no visual clues.

People with **S**ensing (**S**) in their Personality Factor prefer living in the present and handling practical matters, while those with i**N**tuition (**N**) prefer living toward the future and imagining possibilities.

I am usually highly methodical in my working life. I had a manager once who went out of his way to comment on my efficiency and how tidy I kept my desk. Alas, because my natural preference is for i**N**tuition (**N**) this was not replicated at home. I had no desire to pay attention to the sensing tasks of maintaining physical order beyond the necessities. This was also a sticking point for me because it prevented me from inviting people to my home. I felt too embarrassed by my inability to easily organise my home environment. It was too much of a chore to have everything 'display home' tidy so potential visitors would approve. I no longer strive for perfection in my home and accept the way I am. Though even now, the difficulty I have organising my environment still often prevents me from inviting people to my home.

Sensing

- Enjoys handling practical matters.
- Lives in the present, appreciating what's there.
- Like things that are measurable.
- Notices details.
- Likes established routines.

iNtuition

- Enjoys imagining possibilities.
- Lives towards the future foreseeing what might be.

- Likes to be inventive.

- Likes change and variety.

I had a complaint once from a member of the babysitting club I was in. She criticised the fact that I hadn't washed up before she came. Perhaps if she had realised how challenging it had been for me to get myself ready and my three children bathed, fed, and ready for bed before I went out with my husband, she may not have commented, yet it was clearly important to her.

Similarly, I had difficulty explaining to someone with a **S**ensing preference, how to do something or how I knew something but didn't have information to back me up. I don't know how I knew; I just knew. After I found out about my Personality Factor, I had a clearer understanding of why this occurred and learned to trust my knowledge. One time I was totally supported in how I used my i**N**tuitive preference when I told my eleven-year-old son he couldn't do a certain thing when he wanted to go out with his mates. Apart from the obvious, I couldn't explain it further in a way in which he would understand, but I simply didn't want him to partake in the activity. He came home after being with his mates and said, 'I don't know how you knew but it was dangerous, and someone nearly got badly hurt'. Thankfully, he had acknowledged my wish and didn't actively participate with the others.

An area of considerable misunderstanding also takes place between people with a **T**hinking (**T**) versus **F**eeling (**F**) preference. I have found out by knowing my Personality Factor that people with a **T**hinking preference like to deal with facts and objectivity and usually get straight to the point. On the other hand, people with a **F**eeling preference tend to take everything personally, so even when a **T**hinking type says something to a **F**eeling type, which is correct and needs to be said, it could be helpful to say something nice before stating it. Even though I have a preference for **F**eeling, I have learned not to take everything quite so personally; as a result, I no longer feel hurt as often as I did before. There is a misconception that females are the feeling types and males are the thinking types. Interestingly, when it comes to our Personality Factor, approximately half of the population have a preference for **T**hinking and half have a preference for **F**eeling. Not all the **T**hinking types are male, with perhaps 40% being female. With **F**eeling types, the converse is true. Most **F**eeling types are female, with roughly 40% being male.

Thinking

- Prefers to use logic.

- Spontaneously critiques.

- Good at analysing plans.

- Decides with the head.

- Relates to truth and justice.

Feeling

- Prefers to use personal convictions.

- Spontaneously appreciates.

- Good at understanding people.

- Decides with the heart.

- Relates to relationships and harmony.

I have worked with male clients whose Personality Factor included **F**eeling. They had difficulty understanding why they didn't seem to do and want the same things as most of their male counterparts. My female clients, whose Personality Factor included **T**hinking, were at a loss to understand why they didn't seem to be on the same wavelength as most of their female friends.

When it comes to **J**udging (**J**) versus **P**erceiving (**P**), I couldn't understand why my mother-in-law would not drop everything for an impromptu outing invitation, especially if it was her planned washing and ironing day. Me, I could do the washing another day. As a **P**erceiving (**P**) type I enjoy going with the flow and can accommodate interruptions. I now accept and respect my

Judging (**J**) counterparts' need to make plans, so I make careful arrangements if I want to do something with them.

Judging

- Prefers an organised lifestyle.
- Enjoys order and structure.
- Enjoys having life under control.
- Likes handling deadlines and plans in advance.

Perceiving

- Prefers a flexible lifestyle.
- Likes to go with the flow.
- Prefers to experience life as it happens.
- Tends to meet deadlines by a last-minute rush.

While I prefer to go with the flow, I always plan when at work. I remember when I was doing a presentation for someone who I also socialised with. My **J**udging (**J**) type friend was especially surprised when I arrived early to set up. She had warned the group to expect me to be late because I was never on time for social engagements. Knowing my Personality Factor has allowed me to do what is necessary to get the job done, giving me permission to be myself when I have the choice.

We can take on the functions of any Personality Factor we want to. In fact, it is necessary to being well adjusted, effective individuals. However, knowing our Personality Factor can assist in discovering what our preferred functions are and help to determine which tasks become stressful if constantly used. For example, for me the behaviours I display at work are different from those I display at home. People often asked me what my Type is when I run MBTI® workshops. When I ask them to guess, they mostly put forward **E** (**E**xtraversion), **S** (**S**ensing) and **J** (**J**udging). There are varied suggestions for the **T/F** preference.

I am likely to behave as **EST/FJ** to perform the tasks required to conduct the workshops. While I do enjoy running workshops, knowing my Personality Factor helps me understand why they exhaust me. As an **INFP** I manage by pacing myself and not running too many back-to-back sessions.

Be mindful that it is important to maintain a balance by acknowledging your natural talents and using your least preferred functions to help. Remember that in Personality Factor terms, balance means not using your least preferred functions equally or more than your preferred functions. Using your least preferred functions to an equal or greater degree will most likely cause stress. If this occurs over a lengthy period, it is likely to also cause illness.

Balance in Personality Factor terms:

> If you prefer Extraversion, you need Introversion for balance, but not equally or excessively.

> If you prefer Introversion, you need Extraversion for balance, but not equally or excessively.

> If your preference is Sensing, you need iNtuition for balance, but not equally or excessively.

> If your preference is iNtuition, you need Sensing for balance, but not equally or excessively.

> People with a Thinking preference need Feeling for balance, but not equally or excessively.

> People with a Feeling preference need Thinking for balance, but not equally or excessively.

> A Judging preference needs Perceiving for balance, but not equally or excessively.

> A Perceiving preference needs Judging for balance, but not equally or excessively.

If you think about it, society's norm is **ESTJ**. We are generally expected to be friendly and outgoing – **E**xtraversion (**E**). We are expected to follow the rules, pay attention to details, get to work on time, do our tax returns on time, fill in forms – **S**ensing (**S**). It seems more acceptable, be logical and objective, and to deal with the facts – **T**hinking (**T**). It also seems highly regarded to be planned and organised and catch your train on time – **Judging (J)**. It therefore stands to reason that if our Personality Factor does not match society's expectations, then we need to learn about our Personality Factor to provide insights into how we can best navigate our journey through life.

When our natural tendencies and the environmental context are the same, it allows for growth and creativity. My type is **INFP** which is the opposite of **ESTJ**. It makes sense that I may have had more difficulty negotiating my way through my world before I knew about my Personality Factor. I still have trouble dealing with some of society's expectations, however, I no longer feel totally alienated as I have developed strategies to manage most situations.

When our natural tendencies and the environmental context don't match, we can take on all kinds of behaviours as we adapt to the demands of the emerging environmental influences. Knowing my Personality Factor has allowed me to remain true to myself and participate in life without feeling that I am a failure. It also prevented me from continuing down the path of being something that I am not, just so I could fit in.

Temperament Types

Another way to report and discuss our Personality Factor is by describing Temperament Types. This way of looking at Personality Type has its roots in the basic temperament types of Greek mythology. The four Temperament Types attributed to Hippocrates were Choleric, Phlegmatic, Melancholic and Sanguine. Plato later went on to refer to them differently. He named the Choleric temperament, the Idealist character; the Phlegmatic, the Rationalist character; the Melancholic, the Guardian character; and the Sanguine, the Artisan character. David Keirsey in his book *Please Understand Me*, found a direct correlation with Plato's temperament types, in his work on Jung's personality theory. Thus, Keirsey's Temperament Types became **NF** (Idealist), **NT** (Rationalist), **SJ** (Guardian) and **SP** (Artisan).

David Keirsey's Temperament Types offers a more general description of behaviours and a better way to understand others more easily. However, please don't assume another person will behave exactly as predicted in the descriptions. We are all unique and have various levels of adaptation and development. Knowing our Personality Factor and having an awareness of Temperament Types may promote a better understanding of other people and allow us to become better communicators and better problem solvers.

The characteristics presented in the descriptions are key aspects of the temperament pattern. We do things from all four of these styles, however we are more likely to resonate with the one that tends to reflect our natural strengths and talents. If the temperament type pattern you thought would fit you doesn't seem to fit, feel free to explore and find one that fits better.

Can you identify which Temperament Type you are? Have a look at the description for each one and see which one rings true for you.

The Idealist

The Idealist or Catalyst (**NF**) makes up roughly 15% of the population. As an analogy with how our body functions, they are often referred to as the Heart. For them, 'becoming' is most important.

NF's are deeply attuned to people and are naturally empathetic. They can be extremely altruistic. If there is a cause of lasting and deep significance, they'll be there. The danger for them is that they may believe that others should be the same. When **NF**'s become stressed, they need time alone and lots of praise and encouragement.

NF - IDEALIST
Wants to Grow

Values

- Authenticity

- Integrity/identity
- self

Skills

- naturally empathetic
- think people/harmony
- best giver of praise
- attuned to the possibilities of people and institutions

NEEDS

- meaning and significance
- unique identity

STRESS

- Insincerity
- Disharmony

The Rationalist

The Rationalist or Visionary Builder (**NT**) makes up roughly 10% of the population. They may be referred to as the Brains. For them, 'knowing' is most important.

The **NT**'s search is to be able to do all things well. They are good problem solvers and have many ideas. They need staff/helpers to carry out their ideas, though they may have trouble trusting them to do the job properly. Having a problem to solve will lessen the **NT**'s stress.

NT - RATIONALIST
Wants to Know

Values

- competence
- logic
- knowledge
- truth and perfection

Skills

- intellectual ingenuity
- pioneering and predicting
- problem solver

- understands systems

NEEDS

- mastery and self-control
- knowledge and competence

STRESS

- incompetence
- being told what to think

The Guardian

The Guardian or Stabiliser (**SJ**) makes up roughly 45% of the population. They are referred to as the Skeleton. For them 'serving' is most important.

SJ's are sometimes referred to as the salt of the earth. They are very practical and uphold the values of society. They enjoy following the rules and are dedicated to social norms. They run and dominate the armed services, the police force, and financial and government institutions. When **SJ**'s become stressed, let them know they are needed and allow them to serve and earn their keep.

SJ - GUARDIAN
Wants a Place

Values

- belonging
- thrive on social stability
- security

Skills

- attention to detail
- stabilisation of the system
- impartial/patient
- excellent with time, decision making and rules
- dependable

NEEDS

- membership or belonging
- responsibility or duty

STRESS

- disorganisation
- lack of respect for authority

The Artisan

The Artisan or Negotiator/Trouble-Shooter (**SP**) – are roughly 30% of the population. They are referred to as the Nerves. For them 'doing' is most important.

SP's do not like to be tied down, or confined, or obligated. Their motto could be 'Enjoy today because tomorrow never comes!' If **SP**s join the police force, they may invariably become motorbike cops. **SP**'s often work in 'regular' jobs so they can afford to play. They enjoy adventure and extreme sports. To counter stress, **SP**'s need action to restore impulse.

SP - ARTISAN
Wants Spontaneity

Values

- freedom
- action/impact
- spontaneity

Skills

- acute observation
- crisis stimulated

- flexible, realistic

- see things that need to be taken care of

NEEDS

- freedom to act on impulse

- ability to make an impact

STRESS

- rules and hierarchy

- constant routine

I can honestly say that when I have conducted workshops, the people in each session could easily relate to their Temperament Type.

One group (**NF**) loved this and wanted to know more.

The (**NT**) group found it to be a very interesting concept and wanted to do more research.

The (**SJ**) group could really see the practical applications of this knowledge.

While the (**SP**) group said, 'Yep that's so true, when's lunch?'!

NF's like to be liked. As an **NF** I became aware that I subconsciously did things so people would like me. My actions were often misconstrued because of my natural empathy and desire to help people. My motives were often regarded with suspicion by people of differing temperament types. This was a total puzzle to me until I learned about my Personality Factor. I also learned that **NF**'s are the best givers of strokes/praise/empathy and found that I had unrealistic expectations if I thought that I would receive the same from others who were not **NF**'s. It was a real wakeup call for me when I realised that other people are not the same as me and do not want the same things.

Knowing my Personality Factor gave me a most profound insight and cemented my revelation that others also have their own unique set of values. It is not my place to change them because their set of values is equally as important as mine. The most important lesson I learned was that of acceptance. Acceptance that another's way of being and doing things is right for them, just as my way is right for me.

Exploring our Personality Factor is a lifelong developmental process, and many influences can affect the direction of type development. Specific circumstances may also dictate how we behave in different situations. We are all influenced by our environment; have multiple experiences with our home life, our community, and our culture. These all have an impact on how we grow and develop who we are. Life is constantly changing. We are constantly changing. However, I believe we keep our own Personality Factor, with our own unique gifts and our own set of challenges throughout our lives. Fundamentally our true Personality Factor does not change. That doesn't mean that we can't behave in a different manner according to the situation we are in. Growing up with the same home life which offers the same environment does not mean that everyone's Personality Factor develops in the same way. Each person is an individual who is likely to react and develop according to their inherent Personality Factor.

The different components of our psychological type work in interrelated ways to establish balance and effectiveness. According to Carl Jung, Type is a dynamic and complex interrelated system of personality. We also have an order in which we use and develop our four mental functions of **S**ensing, i**N**tuition, **T**hinking and **F**eeling. This order is inborn, and our four-letter description lets us know which function is our number one process. It is called the Dominant function. As we develop, the dominant function is used, and it becomes strengthened and differentiated from the other functions. We tend to have the most skills and conscious use of this function, and we are inclined to trust it the most. We develop this preference to a greater extent than any of the other three. It has the important role of guiding us, being the foundation of our conscious personality.

This number one preference is like the driver of our vehicle. Please indulge me in this analogy of driving cars before the advent of the self-driving car. A car can't go anywhere without a driver, so if we are not using our favourite mental function then it is like trying to drive a car without someone behind the wheel. If there is a passenger in the front, then they can be the navigator. Our second most preferred mental function is our helper. It is called the Auxiliary, and it helps give balance to the dominant function. It doesn't have control over our decisions; however, it is most helpful when making decisions. The auxiliary function is very important in your life but always ranks second in importance to your dominant function.

Our third (Tertiary function) and fourth (Inferior function or least preferred) tend to be less interesting and less well-developed than our dominant and auxiliary functions. We tend to use them less consciously. As you grow and develop, you may learn that there is a time and place to use your third and fourth functions. While your development of these functions tends to occur later in life, you may experience great satisfaction in their development. These lesser favourite preferences are like the passengers in the back seat. They are very useful to look out for clues to pass on to the navigator and the driver during our journey.

The Inferior function, or least well-developed preference, is the opposite of the dominant function. It can provide clues about which areas of your life you wish to avoid and encompasses skills you may have the hardest time developing. Extended use of your Inferior, and your Tertiary functions, tends to require a great deal of energy, thus ongoing use of them may leave you feeling stressed or tired.

While it is not always the case, people generally develop the four functions throughout their lives in the order in which they prefer them. The way you see the world and how you behave tends to change and broaden as you grow and move through life. This happens as you gain experience and develop your four functions. You may spend time later in life developing your tertiary and least-preferred functions. This offers a range of behaviours available to you, and the career and lifestyle options you consider, may change.

We can only imagine how stressful it would be if we tried to drive a car from the passenger seat, or only have the driver travelling alone for long distances. It's the same for our Personality Factor. If we are constantly having to drive the car by ourselves or find that the backseat drivers are doing more than they ought to, it is likely to contribute to high stress levels or even illness. Fundamentally, we need to be the driver of our own vehicle. We also need to listen to our passengers to help us make appropriate decisions for our own wellbeing.

The dominant and auxiliary functions are the core functions of your conscious personality and the basis for much of your self-esteem. Therefore, it is vitally important for us to trust and use our dominant mental functions we are born with. If this doesn't happen, then it may negatively impact our ability to trust our decision-making process or to differentiate and attend to important information in our lives.

Sometimes circumstances such as role expectations (by family and society), financial circumstances, educational background etc can restrict development of our true type. It is never too late to learn about our Personality Factor to help sort out some of the problems we may be having. We can gain this knowledge at any age. I became aware in my late 30's. Other people have discovered their Personality Factor in their 70's.

I am surprised that most people I speak to outside of the corporate arena don't know about the importance of The Personality Factor and the MBTI®. Many of those who do know about it have not gone any further than having completed the questionnaire. They have likely received a short report which is often put away in a drawer because they lack the understanding and knowledge to implement the practical applications of their Personality Factor. The importance and usefulness of knowing their true Personality Factor is often dismissed. Learning more about our Personality Factor will allow us to have an awareness of how other people in our life differ from us. This lets us shift our behaviour and communication and move towards solving problems that may arise in our relationships with our family, friends, partners, children, and work colleagues with much more success and with much less stress.

Personality Type Theory is rich and complex. An in-depth study is needed to truly understand our Personality Factor. You can use your Personality Factor to understand yourself better, to make effective use of your strengths and minimise your challenges. Use it to understand others to allow for better communication. Use it to explore choices of careers, jobs, tasks, situations, or courses of study. Yet, you must be cautious about guessing someone else's type and assuming your guess is correct. It is important to avoid labelling, stereotyping, or limiting other people, as the behaviours we are judging may not be that of their true type. Remember, to be sure of your own Personality Factor, it is important to learn from a qualified MBTI® practitioner who will professionally administer and report on your Personality Factor. Even qualified MBTI® practitioners cannot help you to identify your true Personality Factor without thorough investigation.

Our Personality Factor is fluid. Different behaviours are displayed according to the situation we are in and the environment we may have grown up in. The combinations of the traits and the way the preferences work together can produce huge differences in our behaviours and tendencies. The change of only one letter can make a huge difference in how people with differing Personality Factors see the world. A person with the Personality Factor **ISFP** behaves somewhat differently to someone whose Personality Factor is **INFP** even though there is only one letter different. They have different unique gifts and talents, and they view the world differently and want different things.

I initially didn't report my true type when I first undertook the MBTI®. There were some things in my profile I agreed with but also a lot that were an 'ummm maybe'. When I completed the MBTI® at the time of my marriage breakup, I reported **ISFP**. While parts of this profile suited, a lot didn't. My marriage counsellor told me years later when I caught up with her again, she was very surprised that I continued to go to counselling even though it was often unusual for people with the type I had reported, to seek counselling. Essentially, I scored my adapted type, and after decades of behaving that way, it was a long process to find the real me. It wasn't until I decided to do the MBTI® accreditation that my true type was revealed and everything seemed to fall into place.

Most people agree that we are all different but navigating those differences can be quite challenging at times. At the risk of repeating myself, I must emphasise that the Personality Factor deserves serious consideration in the way we see ourselves in the world. An awareness and understanding of your Personality Factor can be used to navigate through life better as a parent, a friend, a partner, a worker and so on. For me, I now know why I may have difficulty in some things and not in others. It took the pressure off me when I realised that there wasn't anything wrong with me, some things simply weren't my forte. I know what feeds my spirit and what activities are potentially draining and I know what I can do to remedy stressful situations that are within my control.

As I have said previously, not everyone is as interested in the Personality Factor the way I am. Personality Type and the MBTI® isn't a panacea for everything. There are many factors influencing and impacting our lives and everyone's journey is different. Most, however, will see the value in acknowledging the role that Personality can play in navigating life. It could merely lead to a better understanding of yourself, or it could be a very practical tool to assist with relationships, teaching, parenting while better understanding your children, or a way to become more effective at work.

I wish that the useful and insightful role that The Personality Factor plays, be considered in helping to navigate the many and varied experiences encountered on your life's journey. Give yourself permission to be yourself; recognise your strengths; and appreciate the differences in other people.

Chapter Two
The Personality Factor and Parenting

What is your Parenting Style?

I HAVE HAD SEVERAL roles in my life – teaching, counselling, training etc. Still, I believe the most rewarding thing I have accomplished is being a parent.

This chapter is designed to encourage parents to look at themselves and be aware of how their parenting style has a bearing on the way their children might respond in the family environment. The way we think we ought to bring up our children may not be in the best interests of all the children in our care. I believe it is vital for parents to be themselves and parent their way, while at the same time, recognising that their children may have differing needs. Given what we know about the usefulness of The Personality Factor for adults, it also makes sense to use this understanding to identify how our children respond to the world around them, using the strengths and talents they are born with. I want to create an awareness of the need to seriously consider the benefits of knowing and understanding the Personality Factor if you are currently a parent or are thinking of becoming a parent.

If you are a parent:

- Does your child drive you crazy at times?

- Does your child think you are weird?

- Do you give your children what you missed out on, but they don't seem to appreciate it?

- Do you wonder why your children are so different even though you treat them the same?

- Do you and your partner argue about how to bring up your children?

Ever since I was introduced to the MBTI® in the late 1980's, I have explored the use of the Personality Factor in my life. It has been particularly useful to better understand myself. It has also helped considerably in better understanding my children. Through knowing the Personality Factor, I formed an understanding of the nuances of the characteristics and unique gifts we were born with.

Children, too, have different preferences for where their focus lies **E** or **I**; how they take in information and experience life **S** or **N**; how they make decisions **T** or **F**; and whether they prefer routine or flexibility **J** or **P**. Please refer to Chapter 1 for an explanation of the MBTI® terms used.

I'm sure that my children will all have different versions of my parenting style. Nevertheless, (whether they still agree or not remains to be seen), they have all said to me at some time, 'I'm really glad you're my mother' or words to that effect. I have attributed my possible 'good management' to my knowledge and application of the Personality Factor. I know that it has significantly helped me negotiate being a single parent.

Most will agree that children begin learning about themselves from the day they are born. But what if it seems they are born into the wrong family? I have met parents who felt that they must have brought the wrong child home from hospital because he/she wasn't like the rest of the family. Perhaps their children didn't have the same natural preferences as they did. Have you ever wondered why your children may be so different from each other even though you believe you raised them the same way? I am sure many children can relate to feeling that they didn't fit in. I know I felt like that when I was a child, though I didn't understand why until I learned about the Personality Factor.

When parents have children with the same preferences as themselves, they may find they have a special relationship with them. They may see the world in similar ways, so communication is easier, and they tend to want the same things, and may even have the same goals. However, very often there are recognisable differences with some preferences of parents and children. One example comes to mind where both parents have a **J** (**J**udging) preference. They enjoy a decisive, organised approach to life. Both children have a **P** (**P**erceiving) preference, however, and prefer a flexible go-with-the-flow approach to life. If these differences are not acknowledged and accommodated in some way, it could lead to ineffective communication and irreparable differences between the parents and the children. When this happens, it is important to learn to appreciate, value and support each other's perspectives. I believe it is the parent's responsibility to model this appreciation. We need to enjoy and celebrate those differences to avoid serious misunderstandings. Perhaps an awareness, by parents, of the Personality Factor will minimise some of the stress and anxiety experienced by some children these days.

What if your parenting style doesn't cater for your children's needs? When you give your child what you missed out on, how do you know it is for the best? I know parents who have done their utmost to provide things for their children that they believed they themselves missed out on in their childhood. They continually provided activities loved by the parents, whether the child was keen or not. Sometimes influences from family, school and culture do not allow children to develop along their natural paths. For example, children who naturally try to make logical and objective decisions using **T**hinking may be made to feel guilty for not paying enough attention to family harmony and other **F**eeling values, especially if these **F**eeling values are highly regarded by the parents. They may be discouraged from developing their naturally preferred dominant and/or auxiliary functions, and instead be pushed to develop another less-preferred function first. I realise that it is important to provide a range of experiences to produce well-rounded dispositions. However, continually having unrealistic expectations or forcing a child to do a certain activity because you alone value it, may have damaging consequences. I also realise that it is important not to treat all children alike. To be truly fair to each child, they need to be treated as individuals. We can do this by tuning into their differences and needs, and acting accordingly.

For example, I had enrolled my **E** (**E**xtravert) child into after-school care when I was working in a casual job. I used to feel guilty about leaving her there if I wasn't working, so I would pick her up straight after school on those days. She would complain because she wanted to play with her friends. She came home to family members who all preferred **I**ntroversion (**I**). Her two siblings and I prefer **I**ntroversion, so there was no one in the house who was excited about making conversation and doing things with her. She needed these experiences to invigorate her, and I soon realised that I was doing my **E** child a huge disservice by not allowing her to go to after-school care even if I didn't need to send her. Sending her to after-school care served everyone's needs. Sometimes it requires only small adjustments, and my understanding of the Personality Factor helped me work out that as a child with a preference for **E**xtraversion, she needed the company and stimulation that after-school care provided.

I used to think that parenthood is a bit of a conspiracy. Nobody really told me what it is going to be like, perhaps because nobody told them. As parents we have knowledge passed on to us by our own parents either overtly or covertly, and even if we don't totally agree with their methods, we often still find ourselves doing the same thing as our parents.

There is an abundance of books about babies and child development, along with parenting courses available. When my children were born, I don't think they read the manual of life because they didn't seem to do many of the things the parenting books suggested they would do. I also found it difficult to follow through with some of the methods outlined in the books. One thing that was instilled in me from the books and the nurses at the baby clinic, was that babies need to have a routine. As an **INFP** I found it almost impossible to stick to a routine and my children, (two of them especially), did not have the slightest respect for a routine of any sort. I'm sure there are many parents and children who are satisfied with the methods and results discussed in the books. I wasn't one of them and I met many parents, who, like me, felt lost and bamboozled.

So, how do we as parents, bring up happy children and provide for their needs without losing sight of our own needs? How do we gain mutual respect and understanding without allowing our self-esteem, or that of our child, to suffer? This is no easy task I can assure you. Even with my knowledge of the Personality Factor, I found it tough going at times. I do not have all the answers and have continually challenged and questioned my ability to parent.

I can say that from the time I began to understand my own Personality Factor, I became equipped with the confidence to look at the way I raised my children, in a different light. I no longer felt that there was something wrong with me because I wasn't like other mothers. I accepted that I had my own parenting style and was willing to accept responsibility for my choices and actions. I believed in myself, at least as a parent.

Naturally, environmental factors play a vital role in the development of a child's Personality Factor which begins early in life. This development is either enhanced or hindered by the situations we grow up in. If parents can understand their child's unique way of seeing the world, they are more easily able to develop appropriate and effective strategies for nurturing them.

It is vitally important that we use our knowledge to provide the opportunities for growth and development. This will reinforce our children's natural preferences and help them develop those preferences which may challenge them, in a fun non-judging way.

One thing that we are often reliably informed about as parents is that we must praise our children regularly to help build their confidence and self-esteem. These qualities, I believe, are intrinsically linked to the ability to live, learn and grow in an environment of acceptance. While praise is a powerful way to help children develop, one thing I hadn't considered until I discovered the Personality Factor was that not all praise is equal.

I know for myself even as an adult, if I was praised for doing something that I didn't think was overly important, it didn't encourage me to do it more often nor did it make me feel good. I was not impressed when my husband would congratulate me on the tidiness of the house. Although I couldn't understand why I felt so uneasy about it at the time, I see now that it was important to him. On the other hand, I would rather have been congratulated for the creative things I had done with the children that day or just be given a hug for merely being me, and not for the housework I had done.

In a nutshell, **S**ensing children could be praised for their attention to reality; **I**ntuitive children for their creativity; **T**hinking children for their competence; and **F**eeling children for their caring.

It doesn't matter how we may think or feel. Giving praise to children for the tasks or sets of values that they don't believe are important, will not necessarily build self-confidence or make the child feel good. I am not saying that neatness, for example, shouldn't be required. However, praising children for neatness, if it is not important to them, will not have the same positive effect on their self-esteem as praise for some other quality they value. When disciplining children, also consider whether or not the consequence will reward the behaviour we are trying to curb. Sending a child with a preference for **I (I**ntroversion) to their room for bad behaviour, for example, may well support the poor behaviour by giving the child much cherished alone time in their room. Once we work out which rewards work for which children, the appropriate reward can be used as an effective means of managing behaviour.

E (Extraversion) children, who learn best when studying with others, could be rewarded by earning the privilege of having friends visit for a study session. For **I (I**ntroversion) children, allowing them the privilege of working in a quiet space, at a parent's desk for example, may motivate them.

Children with the **S (S**ensing) factor could be given the privilege of engaging in activities which allow their senses to be invigorated. A field trip or building models may serve to motivate the **S** child.

N (i**N**tuitive) children could be rewarded by having the freedom to explore and use their imagination. Encouraging them to imagine their room when it is clean or allowing some interesting plan to rearrange it may motivate them to produce a tidy room.

A reward for a **T** (**T**hinking) child could be supplying them devices and notebooks to help them organise ideas.

F (**F**eeling) children could be rewarded and motivated by allowing them the opportunity to do something they highly value. This may be doing something nice for someone or working closely on an activity with a loved one.

J (**J**udging) children could be motivated by being involved in planning and organising something – a sleepover or an outing for example.

Having some free time to do what they please could be a reward for children with a preference for **P** (**P**erceiving).

Child with a preference for Extraversion	Child with a preference for Introversion
• It is more fun doing something with a group. • I like to have lots of friends. • I really like to talk to people I meet.	• I like doing my favourite activity by myself. • I would rather have a few close friends. • I prefer to keep my thoughts and feelings to myself.

THE PERSONALITY FACTOR

Child with a preference for Sensing	Child with a preference for iNtuition
• It is more fun doing something with things I can see and touch. • I like to start with a plan. • I like to notice the things around me. • I prefer to follow a plan step by step. • I like stories about real people and things.	• I like to imagine things. • I would rather have a few close friends. • I like to create my own plan. • I like to use my imagination. • I enjoy having new ideas. • I prefer make believe stories.

Child with a preference for Thinking	Child with a preference for Feeling
• I notice what needs to be done. • I always ask questions. I always trust my feelings. • I prefer to be right. • It is important to be fair. • It should be done properly the first time.	• I notice that I can help people. • I would rather have a few close friends. • I prefer to be friendly. • I like him because he is kind. • Is it OK to try again?

Child with a preference for Judging	Child with a preference for Perceiving
• I like it better when my day is planned. • I like to plan my journeys. • I often get my homework done early. • It is important to be fair.	• It is much better if I am free to do what I want. • It's fun to explore different things. • I usually leave my homework to the last minute.

In the following Table, I have given a brief description of children's needs and favourite activities according to Temperament Type. I have also included the make-up of my family unit as a single parent. I didn't include my husband in the mix because I didn't know about MBTI® until after our separation.

Children's Temperament Types:

15% of the population NF Idealist – Catalyst	10% of the population NT Rationalist – Inventor
Needs: Relationships, Harmony, Self-understanding Favourite activities may include: • Reading and daydreaming • Acting, role playing, dressing up • Creative writing • Playing music, singing, dancing • Art and craft • Being with nature and people	**Needs:** Competence, Freedom to think, Problems to solve Favourite activities may include: • Music, drama, fine arts • Debating, discussing ideas • Reading and writing poetry • Reading to gain information • Logical games – chess, solving problems
My Family: INFP (Parent) INFP (Child)	**My Family:** INTJ (Child)
30% of the population SP Artisan – Negotiator	45% of the population SJ Guardian – Stabiliser
Needs: Action, Fun, Freedom Favourite activities may include: • Acting, singing, playing music • Drawing, craft • Sports, outdoor activities • Building mechanical things – Lego, Rubik's cubes e.g. • Computer games, gadgets, transformer toys • Magic tricks, comedy	**Needs:** Responsibility, Belonging, Structure and Order Favourite activities may include: • Practical things – cooking, art, craft, making things, fixing things • Physical activities – sport, dancing, athletics • Reading – real life stories especially • Playing a musical instrument • Belonging to groups – e.g., Scouts or Guides. • Collecting things – stamps, rocks, cars
My Family: ESFP (Child)	

Most of the population belong to the **SP** and **SJ** groups combined, though only one of my family members out of four fits into this group. From a society viewpoint, three of us (**NF, NT, NF**) are in the minority, while within our family, one member (**SP**) felt perhaps that she didn't completely belong there. This perspective has helped me understand the dynamics in my family, as I endeavoured to do the best I could for everyone, including myself.

Because their Personality Factor appears to be constantly validated by society expectations, I wonder if parents who belong to the **SP** and **SJ** groups and who have offspring of a similar Personality Factor to theirs, struggle to understand what all the fuss is about from some parents, like me, who have different temperaments. They may question why we seem to find it so challenging to raise our children in the same way that many others find effective.

It is interesting to me that no one in my family belongs to the **SJ** group. It seems we all fight against following social norms to some degree. I certainly struggled in my own family growing up. I can see now that no one has the same Personality Factor as I do. Nobody even has the same Temperament. I didn't have anyone to relate to or anyone who viewed things the way I did. I grew up taking my cues from the household members around me. My family consists of my parents and my five siblings. I am the eldest child. I share the **F** (**F**eeling) preference with one other sibling. However, we are different Temperament types. I am the odd one out. The other members of my family share similar Personality Factors and are more able to inherently relate to each other. I learned what was acceptable and what was not. I often felt frustrated, and I can see now that I began to mimic those values prized by my parents and siblings. I adapted to fit in and be accepted. I believe I made choices based on what the rest of the family thought was important rather than what was right for me.

A continuation of this practice was shown in my choosing a husband who was very similar to the rest of my family. I found myself believing I was someone different right into my thirties, until I came across the MBTI®. At the time of my marriage break up, around age thirty-five, I reported my adapted type, **ISFP**. A combination of family influences and societal expectations moulded me into behaving as a **S**ensing type. It wasn't until much later, after deep soul searching which led me to undertake my MBTI® accreditation, that I discovered I am an **INFP**. I still struggle to 'find my flock' at times. Yet my knowledge and understanding of my Personality Factor has allowed me to accept that I am not the same as most people I meet, and that it is OK.

It seems that there are many parenting programs available to help parents, and all appear to offer valid approaches for raising children. I wonder, however, whether they are mostly written from the point of view of the author. They seem to propose strategies which are right for them, and it looks as if they expect that they will work for every child. They do provide helpful strategies, and many parents find them valuable. However, I am constantly mindful that the Personality Factor of the child may not have been taken into consideration. Also, if the Personality Factor of the parent differs from that of the author, then that parent may have difficulty carrying out the suggestions outlined. I know that collecting stickers for tasks with rewards after a certain target is reached is a very popular motivator. I also know that I found it very challenging to maintain regularity and consistency so inevitably the whole project would fall apart. I'm not sure that all my children were motivated by this activity either. I had to find other approaches which suited us all better.

My **ESFP** daughter (third child) seemed to do more of what the books said. She was a 'model' baby until she was about six weeks old. When she noticed the world around her, there was no stopping her. As a child with **E**xtraverted **S**ensing as her dominant preference, she wanted to explore the world. She crawled at five months and walked at nine months.

As the odd one out in this family, I believe that my **ESFP** child has also struggled to find someone in the family who understands her. She said to me in her late teens/early adulthood, 'I'm so glad you let me be who I am'. She was meeting other people at university who had told her they had difficult relationships with their parents, especially their mothers. They felt they couldn't be themselves and didn't meet the expectations their mothers had of them. They were envious that she had a mother who at least let her be who she was. I am very grateful that my knowledge of the Personality Factor has at least permitted this to happen. It was not easy, and without this knowledge we could have regularly been at inexplicable loggerheads. Things could have become very ugly. She has a very different Personality Factor to me and to her siblings and may still be searching for an understanding and connection that she craves from her family.

My **INFP** daughter (second child) has always been good at language and spoke in sentences at age two and a bit. After a shaky start straight out of high school, she worked towards getting into an area of study which would fulfil her and is currently a well-respected practitioner in her field. I have also found among my treasures, many more notes from her than from the others saying how much she appreciates me. Once, she came home from a friend's house when she was about nine years old and said to me, 'I'm really glad I chose you as my mother'. She possibly had a 'knowing' that we have the same Personality Factor so life with me seemed 'comfortable'. We are both **INFP**.

On the other hand, as a young child my first born (son) always wanted to know about the world. He wanted to be competent in everything and became frustrated if things were not how he needed them to be. He drove me crazy asking 'why' much more than the other two did. Even though we share the **I** (**I**ntroversion) and the **N** (i**N**tuition) factors, as an **INTJ** it was most likely frustrating for him at times, having me as a parent. We clashed regularly on the **T-F** (**T**hinking-**F**eeling) and the **J-P** (**J**udging-**P**erceiving) preferences (I am **INFP**). His need for logic and my largely non-logic nature are still causes of many misunderstandings. However, my understanding of the differences allowed me to cease beating myself up because we didn't see eye to eye at times.

He may have wished for a mother who did everything for him, (that was not my forte), so he could get on with other pursuits. However, after he left home to go to university he said, 'I know your methods have been a bit different, but they've worked, thanks. I look around and see some of my friends and I don't know how they'll cope when they leave home'.

While there have been many challenges being a single parent, I was buoyed by some comments from a parent in one of my workshops. She said that I was lucky to parent by myself because I didn't have a differing parenting style to deal with. I hadn't considered that before, so I immediately stopped feeling sorry for myself and revelled in the fact that I could parent with acceptance and flexibility. I was excited to be able to use different styles for different children and I didn't have to argue with someone who didn't understand what I was trying to achieve.

My conviction to understand and use my Personality Factor to help me raise my children was cemented when I met prominent author and proponent of using Personality Type with children, Dr Elizabeth Murphy. I felt extremely privileged when I had the opportunity to drive Elizabeth around to various venues used for the MBTI® Conference in 1996 in Brisbane, Australia.

Dr Murphy has been working with personality type for children since the early 1980's. Since then, she has won many awards for her contribution to type in education. She is the author of *The Developing Child* and is the co-author of the Murphy-Meisgeier Type Indicator for Children (MMTIC®).

She signed my copy of her book and since then her work has reinforced for me the concept that children are born with special talents and strengths. They have their own way of seeing things.

I quickly realised that my children were not displaying certain behaviours just to irritate me (well maybe sometimes they were). They merely have their own way of seeing and doing things which are different to mine.

THE PERSONALITY FACTOR

The Developing Child

'*Thank you for spending the day with me and helping me get from place to place. I wish you well as you continue your awareness of differences to improve relationships with children.*'

It is not the same world now as it was when I was bringing up my children. Having said that, about twenty-five years ago I wrote down some notes about some of the challenges encountered by parents and teachers. These distractions included things like technology, computers, computer games, the Internet, media, TV, and advertising; parents pushing their children too hard too soon to achieve; children forgetting how to play and how to communicate; children growing up knowing more than their parents.

I could write the same things now. However, looking back, compared with today most of those challenges were just that, distractions. The immediate influences and consequences of social media and our reliance on technology are causing increased pressures on everyone. Parents are now faced with similar challenges that I was, only they appear to be magnified.

At present, unrelenting challenges to our self-worth and that of our children are escalating at an alarming level and we need all the help we can get. I believe it is more important than ever to consider our Personality Factor and that of our children. We can add this wisdom to our arsenal of resources and therapies when making our decisions about how we can best support them and remain true to ourselves.

We cannot change what we may have done in the past. However, we can use this new understanding of our Personality Factor to become better parents, or perhaps help our children become better people. We can encourage our children to develop their own potential and hopefully they will not fall into the same traps and make the same mistakes we, or our parents, may have done.

Based on my insights and personal experience, I have found that knowledge of the Personality Factor can significantly help parents increase self-esteem and reduce stress for their children. There is a lot of emphasis these days placed on teaching children to be resilient. However, I believe resilience is different for different children. Of course, world events that are beyond our control may cause stress in children. Then again, by not understanding our children and not providing them with some of their needs that may not coincide with our own parenting style, we face the risk of further contributing to their potentially high stress levels. In my opinion, it may be as simple as understanding that some children like hugs and some don't; that some children need company while others are more independent; that some children respond well to strict routines while others don't; some are more practically minded, and others are not.

One of the most important issues I discovered is that there is no right or wrong way to parent, except to be who you are. What works for me will not necessarily work for you. Whatever we do, it is the best we can do with the knowledge we have. If we are lucky, our family shares similar Personality Factors allowing a special understanding that comes from viewing the world in similar ways. If our family seems to have some areas of contention, we can use the Personality Factor to have an awareness of our children's differences and nurture happy, effective human beings.

I love this. All this Personality Factor stuff energises me, and I am passionate about finding solutions for discovering everyone's true potential. I also know that this level of commitment is not for everyone. I am sure that we are all primarily concerned with making our children feel good about themselves by recognising their strengths and talents. Similarly, I am confident that most parents will acknowledge that understanding their children's differences will have a beneficial influence on their growth and happiness.

Clearly, children must live in our world. They need to learn how to navigate their growth within the family they are in, and there are lessons to be learned. However, an understanding of differences and consideration of the impact that knowledge of the Personality Factor can have, may do wonders towards bringing up healthy well-rounded humans without losing yourself in the meantime.

How do we find out about our children's Personality Factor?

The fact remains – our child's personality does affect how they behave and respond to our parenting methods. So how can we determine our child's personality type and how can we adjust our methods of parenting to provide a nurturing environment for all?

One way of working out your child's Personality Factor is to know your own. With an understanding of the personality type functions, you can read the descriptors of each preference to see if you can work out your child's Personality Factor. Please make sure you are provided with professional feedback and receive a full profile from a reputable MBTI® provider when finding out about your own Personality Factor. It may only confuse matters if you simply do a quick online questionnaire to receive a four-letter result without any in-depth follow-up.

I have to say, there currently appears to be very few MBTI® practitioners who specialise in the children's version of the MBTI® – it is called the Murphy-Meisgeier Type Indicator for Children (MMTIC®). There are, however, some excellent online resources available at www.peoplestripes.org and https://elizabethmurphymmtic.com/.

As parents, we need to be who we are while appreciating the differences in our children. We can then provide the support necessary for our children to accomplish essential tasks for healthy growth and development, for them.

Give yourself permission to be yourself and appreciate the differences in your children. Allow them to be who they are, and not simply try to create images of you.

Chapter Three

The Personality Factor and Teaching

This chapter is about my experience working in schools and offers a message to teachers. My wish is to provide an awareness to teachers that the way they impart their skills may or may not be in the best interests of all the children in their care.

Over four decades ago, I graduated from Teachers College with a spring in my step and hope in my heart. Since then, I have taught in primary and secondary schools in Queensland and New South Wales. Most recently, I was engaged as a school counsellor/welfare teacher in primary and secondary schools. Students were often referred to me for learning difficulties or behavioural problems. I assisted teachers with developing a plan of action to help them. In many cases I could see a link between a mismatch in the expectations of both teacher and student and the problems that presented because of their differing Personality Factors.

I also found that many teachers were struggling to find the answer to engaging their pupils effectively, especially in the primary schools. They were looking for other ways to enhance their teaching methods. The Personality Factor can help to reflect on how teaching style impacts the way children may respond in the classroom. It is important for teachers to be themselves and teach to their strengths. However, depending on their Personality Factor, not all students may respond favourably to the teacher's individual style.

We know that early educational experiences are vital for forming habits for successful lifelong learning. However, it is important to understand that children, like adults, have preferred ways of learning.

I acknowledge that there are many factors which affect the performance of children at school. However, considering the Personality Factor of teachers and of students may assist in part with the struggle teachers often have engaging their charges. To coin a phrase, 'if you can reach them, you can teach them'.

If you are a teacher:

- Have you ever questioned why some of your students just don't seem to understand what you are trying to teach them?

- Do some of your students seem to drive you to distraction at times?

- Do you have students who constantly chatter in class?

- Have you wondered why you may have some students in your class with poor behaviour and diminished academic achievement despite their high level of intelligence?

How often have we considered that our teaching style may be helpful for some students but not for others? As revealed in the previous chapter, understanding the Personality Factor can have a considerable impact on how parents raise their children. If teachers had this understanding, they may be able to provide feedback to parents while respecting the child's preferences. They could use this knowledge to adjust their strategies to cater to their students' learning needs more appropriately.

I will be using the type descriptors in Chapter 1 to illustrate the fact that differing Personality Factors may have some bearing on how teachers 'teach'.

Clash between teaching style and learning style

As teachers, we all know that each child in our class is different with differing needs. Navigating those differences and providing the best possible care is a huge challenge. A knowledge of the Personality Factor can most certainly help teachers pinpoint some of those differences instead of offering random strategies in the hope that they could help some students. The Personality Factor can provide a framework for lesson design that accommodates all learning approaches.

As a primary teacher of younger grades who prefers **Extraversion**, you may highly regard those children who come to school ready to do 'show and tell' or 'morning talks' and perform confidently. Those children most likely also have a natural preference for **Extraversion** so their ability to articulate effortlessly indeed comes easily. While they are regularly praised for their performance, those with a natural preference for **Introversion** might struggle with talking in front of the class and may be marked down for their perceived lack of ability due to their natural reserve. Even a teacher with a preference for Introversion may value the ability of the extraverted child over one who is more tentative when doing 'show and tell', especially if they don't know about the Personality Factor. A parent with a similar preference, for example, may see their child's preference for **Extraversion** as a positive attitude, allowing them to be socially adjusted. A teacher with a different preference may see it as seemingly unproductive and disruptive.

My third child, who has a preference for **Extraversion**, came home with glowing remarks about her ability to talk in front of the class and engage in conversation on her report card in Grade 1. Because I have knowledge of the Personality Factor, I knew she had a natural ability for this. I would have been more impressed if she had been given these comments as a child who preferred Introversion. When parents understand the Personality Factor, they may be able to see that a teacher's point of view may only reflect his or her own preferences, and not a rejection of their child.

When teachers understand the Personality Factor, they may well adjust their teaching strategies and their interpretation of behaviours in the classroom. In the classroom, even an understanding by teachers of the difference between the learning styles of students with **E**xtraversion and **I**ntroversion, may have an illuminating effect on how they manage their classrooms. Those students with a preference for **E**xtraversion can often get into trouble for talking. However, they do their best work when talking with others, although they need some alone time at first to think about the task. These students are generally enthusiastic, have high energy and seem chatty but to a teacher with a preference for **I**ntroversion and no knowledge of the Personality Factor, they may appear overwhelming, lacking listening skills and taking up a lot of time in the classroom with their need for action and verbalising.

While **I**ntroverts often get into trouble for not verbally participating, they do their best work by themselves. They do, however, need to discuss the task with others to gather ideas. With

Introverts, you may not see what they have to offer if they are not encouraged to speak up. **I**'s usually think before they speak, are quiet and are often wired to be diligent students. To a teacher with a preference for **E**xtraversion and no knowledge of the Personality Factor, they could be overlooked, appear slow or disinterested and hard to assess as their talent may be well hidden.

In my work as a school counsellor, I regularly had referrals for 'poor' behaviour in the classroom. I acknowledge that various factors are in play when it comes to classroom management. However, I could see that much of the poor behaviour came about because the teacher did not recognise the differences in their own and their students' Personality Factor. They did not know how to engage some of their students in learning because of the expectations they had from their own Personality Factor.

While an understanding of the Personality Factor is not a panacea for all the challenges faced by teachers in the classroom, it can go a long way towards knowing yourself as a teacher and can assist with engaging students more successfully. Using the knowledge gained, a more targeted approach may be used, catering to students' needs, rather than rejecting them and labelling them with an affliction because they do not hold the same values as you do.

Without even a basic inkling of how the Personality Factor can help, teaching in schools may be a bit of a hit and miss affair, despite the considerable effort made by all members of the school community. If we look at the learning styles of the temperaments discussed in the previous chapter, and the distribution of the Personality Factors of students and teachers in the schools, we can see that there is a huge chunk of the school population that may not be adequately catered for or engaged in learning.

What is your Learning Style?

The NF Student

You could call this group the *creative idealists*.

These students typically make up around 15% of the school population.

The **NF** student likes to communicate in a personal way with others. This need seems to be frequently catered for when they first go to school. Teachers tend to spend a lot of time engaging in personal communication during the Early Learning Education years. By the time students participate in high school education, the direct personal interaction between student and teacher is vastly reduced and almost lost.

Because of their dislikes for insincerity and disharmony, **NF** students can be almost hypersensitive to conflict and may even become physically ill when exposed to this sort of tension. Their talents lie in communication skills and their ability to speak may be far beyond their capacity to write their thoughts down.

During my brief time working as a counsellor in a high school, I saw more **NF** students than any of the other types. Most of those self-referred, often to discuss their personal distress over events happening around them. Quite often it was about perceived injustices occurring in the classroom or among friendship groups.

Interestingly to me, a substantial number of **NF** students were referred by teachers because of poor attitude and disruptive behaviour. This regularly occurred, possibly because of the **NF** student's need for meaning and harmony, and personal communication. In each case there appeared to be a conflict between the student and the referring teacher, most likely due to a difference in their Personality Factor along with the increasingly impersonal way in which high schools seem to operate. The **NF** student may quickly disengage and become disruptive when this happens. To them it is personal.

The NT Student

These students might be called the *creative thinkers*.

As a student, the **NT** learner may neglect other school subjects while pursuing particular inspirations. This may lead to failed grades in those neglected subjects. Because of their need to be competent in all things, their work is never finished.

These students are keen to share ideas with their intellectual peers. Often the **NT** student may wish to establish this communication with teachers if they cannot find this attribute amongst their classmates. This isolation from peers can result in these students' becoming outsiders.

As a group, they make up around 10% of the school population but I saw a higher number than expected of **NT** students in my school counselling role.

While one student self-referred, teachers referred the others. The reasons for referral included students being stressed out because they thought that they were not doing well enough, and for not handing in assignments. Their desire to go off on a tangent to delve into other interesting things often lead to missing deadlines.

Another reason for referral was that the students did not seem to understand social expectations. They often felt uneasy around their more popular peers and didn't know how to be accepted by the group. Only the student who self-referred continued to come to counselling for help with ongoing social concerns.

The SJ Student

These students may be referred to as the *responsible* group who want to *belong*.

The **SJ** student seems to fit into most classrooms better than other temperament. According to well documented studies, this could be, in part, because most classrooms are organised by teachers with an **SJ** temperament. Teachers with the **SJ** temperament occur in the profession more than all the other temperament types put together. These students like to know that they are doing the right thing and are contributing to upholding the operating procedures of the school.

They are almost the model students as they generally have good study habits and wish to please the teacher by having their homework and assignments done on time. Given that the **SJ** students occur in the school population in greater numbers than the other types, it is noteworthy that only 7% of the students I saw were **SJ**. It may be that they are the group which is most likely to be consistently engaged in classroom learning because their needs are more often met in most school environments.

The **SJ** students I saw were referred by teachers, for problems at home and learning difficulties in some subject areas, especially the less factual and practical ones. It may be possible that the delivery of lessons in high school are self-directed and research oriented, rather than step by step instructions with clear expectations preferred by the **SJ** student.

The SP Student

We could refer to this group as the *needing action* group.

These students make up around 30% of the school population. However, teachers with an **SP** temperament are the least represented amongst the teacher population, making up around 4% of the numbers of teachers in schools.

Thus, the unique learning style of the **SP** student is often not catered for as a matter of course in most classrooms. They are also the most likely to drop out of school or get a job rather than go on to institutions of higher learning.

For them, the methods of testing for knowledge used in many school settings, rarely suits **SP** students as they are more practically oriented. This may lead to a low correlation between academic ability and exam results.

My **SP** daughter did not enjoy high school and left school after Year 10. She worked in hospitality and did some TAFE courses for a few years. Later she enrolled in a four-year university course as a mature age student and excelled in an area of interest to her.

Most of the **SP** students I saw were referred to me for school refusal and disruptive behaviour. A few were referred because of the stress caused by having to sit the HSC (Higher School Certificate) in year 12. I would not have expected to see **SP** students self-refer. However, I believe those who did come to see me perhaps saw it as a way of avoiding going to their classes.

It seems to me that the mismatch between an **SP**'s temperament and teaching practices in many schools, contributes in no small way to the disruptive behaviours and poor attendances reported. Is it possible that children with the typical **SP** temperament are deemed to be disruptive to classroom proceedings? Do they elicit a referral for intervention because they do not conform to the classroom requirements of some teachers?

Learning Styles for each Temperament Type:

15% of the population. **NF Student** *Catalyst*	10% of the population. **NT Student** *Inventor*
Requires: Relationships-Harmony-Self-understanding **Learning Style** • Imaginative, innovative • Focuses on the future • Catalyst for growth and development • Authentic, empathic • Trusts inspirations and imagination • Works to develop potential in others **Needs:** • Meaning • Identity • Harmony • Uniqueness **Dislikes:** • Insincerity • Disharmony	**Requires:** Competence-Freedom to think-Problems to solve **Learning Style** • Analytical, inventive • Focuses on the future • Independent thinker • Seeks justice and fairness • Asks why? Why not? What if? • Work often involves strategic planning and design **Needs:** • Competence • Intellectual freedom • Mastery • Achievement **Dislikes:** • Incompetence • Being told what to think
30% of the population. **SP Student** *Artisan - Negotiator*	45% of the population. **SJ Student** *Investigator*
Requires: Action-Fun-Freedom **Learning Style** • Realistic, factual • Focuses on the present • Natural negotiator and trouble-shooter • Spontaneous, acts on impulse • Likes movement and hands-on activity • Work is often tactical – gets the job done **Needs:** • Freedom • Action • Fun • To make an impression **Dislikes:** • Rules and Hierarchy • Routine	**Requires:** Responsibility-Belonging-Structure and order **Learning Style** • Responsible, dependable • Focuses on the past, the way things have been done • Logistical, practical • Trusts what is known from experience • Works to maintain institutions and order **Needs:** • Structure and order • Belonging • Responsibility **Dislikes:** • Disorganisation • Lack of respect for authority

Way back in the early 1990's when it was not a requirement to remain at school until 17 years of age, I worked with long-term unemployed youth. I was so enthusiastic about the Personality Factor, that I had to curb my desire to overload these young people with insights into their psyche. They certainly did not want that. They were teenagers who pretty much knew who they were, and they were right, according to them. Mostly they were right, but they could not get past their clash with authority, which was then the CES (Commonwealth Employment Service). The fact that most had dropped out of school and did not have qualifications also stood in the way of getting jobs. The majority were from the **SP** Temperament group which is the group most likely to discontinue with school and be the most streetwise. It made it hard for them to reconcile the expectations of the CES, which was paying them an unemployment benefit, and their desire to be true to their own Personality Factor.

I used my expertise to assist them with finding employment. Apart from helping to see that their frustrations were real, I was able to use my knowledge of the Personality Factor to contribute to their obtaining gainful employment more suited to them. It was so powerful that when I gave them a brief printout of their profile, I had teenage boys, who were not the least bit interested in the Personality Factor, say to me, 'Yep. This is me. I'm going to put this up on my wall!'.

At another time, while I was conducting my private counselling business, I had some parents come to me for advice about their son who was finishing Year 10 and who didn't want to continue to complete Years 11 and 12. It was highly regarded at that time, to finish Year 12, and most likely go to university. Of course, this is what the parents wanted for their son, and they could not understand why he was so disinterested in school. Perhaps they needed confirmation that there was another pathway for him. Remember, this was before the time when there were many other opportunities to do school-based traineeships and such.

After investigating the Personality Factor of all concerned, it was seen that they all viewed things differently. The son had an **SP** preference which was different from that of his parents. He was suited to a more practical, hands-on vocation. I advised that getting an apprenticeship or doing a TAFE course would be viable options instead of continuing a more academic pathway. These options addressed the issue of school refusal and catered to the son's strengths and abilities. The danger of continuing to finish Year 12 was that if he didn't want to pursue a university education, he was likely to become unemployable. He would have been an unskilled worker at the age of eighteen when you could employ someone younger with the same skills for cheaper rates of pay. The value of using the Personality Factor in this situation was that it provided a way to explain to the parents how to best cater for their son's needs as well as providing an insight to the parents about their own expectations.

I am heartened to know that selected schools now take the Personality Factor into consideration especially when assisting their students choose career pathways and make choices of subjects in high school, but many still do not. However, it may now be more important than ever for students to make appropriate choices for their futures by knowing their Personality Factor.

What is your Teaching Style?

NF Teachers

Making up around 32% of teachers in schools, they tend to have a prolonged stay in teaching. Their favourite teaching areas include humanities, social sciences, theatre, music, foreign languages, speech and theology. Their favourite instructional techniques include group projects, interaction, discussion, shows, simulations and games.

Teachers with the **NF** Temperament are moderately represented in schools, so those **NF** students are well-catered for, especially in the primary schools where classrooms tend to operate in a more personable way. I have already mentioned that this personal approach may be mostly lacking in secondary schools.

NF students want personal expressions of appreciation and enjoy having their ideas and feelings understood by others. Unfortunately for those students, this is most likely to be understood only by the **NF** teachers. **NF** students do not appreciate impersonal treatment of themselves or others especially if it involves their friends, whether their friends need this personal treatment or not.

NT Teachers

NT teachers are likely to have a medium stay in teaching and make up roughly 8% of the teaching population. Their favoured teaching areas are likely to be philosophy, science, technology, mathematics and linguistics. Their favoured instructional techniques include lectures, tests, compositions, projects and reports.

Neither **NT** students nor **NT** teachers are found in substantial numbers in most schools. You are more likely to find a higher percentage of **NT** students and teachers or lecturers in higher learning institutions like universities. In primary schools there are fewer **NT** teachers. **NT** teachers do not appreciate anything which violates logic, reason, or principle, although many of these things are on the agenda in most schools run in an **SJ** style. Unlike the **SJ** teacher, they are not impressed by being commended by routine tasks well done; and they do not appreciate it when rules or traditions get in the way of thorough research and maximum results.

SJ Teachers

The **SJ** teacher makes up roughly 56% of the schools' population and they invariably have a prolonged stay in teaching. Most may be found in primary schools, while their favoured subject areas in secondary schools include clerical, business, technological and applied studies, history and geography. Their preferred instructional techniques include recitation, drills, composition, tests, quizzes and demonstrations.

The typical school has more **SJ** teachers than any other temperament. It makes sense then that the general organisation and running of the school is most likely conducted in an **SJ** style, so the **SJ** teachers are well catered for. **SJ** teachers appreciate it when they are praised for thoroughness and accuracy and like to be commended for their loyalty, responsibility and industriousness even though they may be shy in receiving it. They may not appreciate deadlines not being met or other teachers not using standard operating procedures. Speaking for myself, this organisational style may not suit all students, and it also may not suit all teachers. I certainly found that my experience in the school system didn't suit me right from the beginning of my teaching career.

THE PERSONALITY FACTOR

I remember back in the day, during my second year of teaching, I was required to pass an Inspection so that I could become a permanent teacher. The School Inspector sat at the back of the classroom with the lesson plan I had prepared. During the lesson I realised that the students did not understand what I was trying to teach them, so I changed my method of instruction mid lesson, hoping for a better outcome. After the lesson, the School Inspector took me to task for not following my lesson plan. I found it difficult to adhere to the expectations that the school system had of me, so I resigned in my third year of teaching. I was living in a country area with my husband who was also teaching. I didn't really know myself well enough then, and there were very few options available to me, so a short time later I returned to teach in the school I had left as they couldn't find another person willing to come to a remote area to replace me.

I resigned again after six years of teaching when my first child was born. While I did go back into teaching after some time away working in other employment sectors, my learning about the Personality Factor helped me to understand why there was a mismatch between my methods and those mostly required by the schools I worked in. It gave me an insight as to how I could manage myself while performing my duties as a teacher throughout the rest of my career.

SP Teachers

Teaching is rarely chosen as a career amongst those with an **SP** Temperament, making up only about 4% of the teaching population. They mostly have a short stay in teaching because their favoured teaching areas being arts and crafts, sports, drama, music and recreation are not generally supported in most school systems. They prefer projects, contests, games and demonstrations as their instructional techniques.

The numbers of **SP** students in most schools are almost the same as **SJ**'s. The point is that teachers with the **SP** preference are underrepresented. This creates a huge gap between the learning styles of the **SP** students and the number of teachers who are sympathetic to their learning needs. For **SP** teachers, the process is more important than the product. **SP** teachers also do not appreciate being told how to work, nor do they appreciate standard operating procedures. You could see how a potential clash between **SP** teachers and school administration may come about, perhaps leading to fewer **SP** teachers in schools.

Teaching Styles for each Temperament Type:

32% of the teaching population. **NF Teacher** Prime Value in teaching is growth of **identity and integrity.** **Long stay** in teaching.	**8%** of the teaching population. **NT Teacher** Prime Value in teaching is growth of **knowledge and skills.** **Medium stay** in teaching.
4% of the teaching population. **SP Teacher** Prime Value in teaching is growth of **spontaneity and freedom.** **Short stay** in teaching	**56%** of the teaching population. **SJ Teacher** Prime Value in teaching is growth of **responsibility and utility.** **Long stay** in teaching

Using The Personality Factor in Schools

It seems clear to me that the current school system does not suit all children to the same degree. There are a range of factors which may contribute to a child not achieving in school. Teachers know that the children in their class have different circumstances and diverse needs, although many teachers are at a loss as to what to do about this. I know that the schools and their support services do an admirable job of providing assistance to children in need of help, though very rarely is the Personality Factor considered. Throughout my work in schools as a teacher and a school counsellor, I have seen numerous situations where an understanding of personality, both the student's and the teacher's, could have helped in lessening frustrations and assisted in solving the problems encountered. As a school counsellor/student welfare officer in remote communities, I was able to use my knowledge of the Personality Factor to assist where I could. With the students who were referred to me for various problems in the classroom, I could often see a link between the teacher's perceived problem and the student's learning style not being catered for.

Teachers and parents may need to remember that teenagers always think they are right. Well, in Personality Factor terms, they often are – for them. They usually know who they are. Unfortunately, they mostly don't have the maturity to appreciate that there are people amongst their peers and of course parents and teachers, who have different Personality Factors and see things differently.

My input by looking at their Personality Factor proved helpful for the students. Remember, I knew that the teachers at the schools I worked in were not familiar with the Personality Factor so the insights gained could only be used by the students themselves. They couldn't change other people such as their peers or teachers, but they were better able to understand themselves and improve relationships with teachers, parents and friends. I noticed that the students I saw had a greater sense of self than I ever did. They knew who they were and what they wanted – there is power in that, but they didn't know how to use that power. The Personality Factor certainly contributed to better self-management among these students, as well as an understanding of the personality differences of some of their peers.

If teachers learn and apply the Personality Factor concepts, they may understand how their own Personality Factor will influence what they see as the right way to teach and learn. These insights will most certainly lead them to better accommodate the variations between individual students, offering differing options for learning. Knowing the Personality Factor will indeed have implications for the students, far beyond school. Knowledge of the Personality Factor may assist in structuring instructions and assignments. It could help by adapting assessments to measure learning more accurately and cater for differentiating learning styles. These strategies may then contribute to better classroom participation consequently enriching student/teacher interactions. Using this model in schools may also help teachers (and parents) understand the variety of options available to help learners manage their learning styles and reach their objectives. Identifying a student's individual strengths may invariably lead to strengthened self-esteem, enhanced achievement and better social interaction skills.

Identifying those things which do not come naturally will allow students and teachers to recognise which tasks will require them to adjust. They could be those which take more energy and may initially be more difficult. This knowledge will help students persevere with the task rather than giving up, and they might not feel like they are failing. It may provide more effective studying techniques and help with finding ways to stay focused when faced with challenging tasks. When all this happens, students are likely to be less stressed. Once again, I emphasise that there is a wide range of factors which may produce underachieving and poorly behaved students. Also, the number of students I saw was a small percentage of the student body in schools. However, my work has shown that if individual learning needs are not met, the students may become tired, restless, sad, stressed or badly behaved.

A personal example of this is when my son was in Year 7 in the 1980's. There was an incident at school which was easily sorted out because of my knowledge of the Personality Factor. As a teacher, it was often considered that communication with a parent was necessary if a student came to school 'out of sorts'. In this case the reverse was true. My son was regularly coming home in a foul mood so I wondered if there may be something going on at school which was causing this irregular behaviour. I finally got to the bottom of it. As an **NT** student he was frustrated and bored in maths especially, because the teacher kept going over and over the same thing until he could be sure that everyone in the class knew it. After speaking with the teacher, I found that my son didn't bother to offer up the answer, so the teacher had no confirmation he knew it. I spoke to the teacher about the Personality Factor and after a few days of more careful observation, the teacher admitted that there were more students than my son who were also bored. My intervention with the knowledge I had resulted in this small group of students being given enrichment work to challenge them more. My son came home each day with a cheerful disposition because he was now being better catered for in the classroom.

Some behaviours are of course cause for concern and may indeed require in depth specialist investigation; however, I suggest that looking at the Personality Factor first may circumvent the taxing of sometimes scarce professional resources needed otherwise.

A teacher's Personality Factor undoubtedly influences the nature of the classroom environment. This following extract from a study in the Journal of Psychological Type volume 18, 1989., page 55 and 56, says it all for me.

> *'A teacher's personality influences the nature of the classroom environment as perceived by students. While teachers have no control over student intelligence and how much students learn as a result, they do have control of the environment they create in the classroom and its effect on student learning. It has long been recognised by teacher educators that certain teachers create an environment not conducive to*

learning. But what to do about it was not always clear. In understanding personality type theory, teachers at all levels can begin to understand cause and effect in the classroom and begin to diagnose and analyse behaviours that reduce learning.'

There is a vast amount of material available about personality and learning styles, and strategies to modify classroom instruction to cater for student differences. However, after over thirty years of using the Personality Factor and having more recently spent time in schools as a school counsellor, I am at loss to understand why more notice isn't taken of the role personality may play in effective teaching and overall understanding of students.

Having said that, I am not sure how this can be achieved in the current school systems. There are already specialist teachers who assist underachieving students in most schools. Is it possible that they, or another interested, dedicated staff member, undertake certification to administer and interpret the MBTI® (Myers-Briggs Type Indicator) and/or the MMTIC® (Murphy-Meisgeier Type Indicator for Children) to address the Personality Factor.

Understanding our Personality Factor may help us become better teachers. We can give ourselves permission to be ourselves, without losing sight of our own needs. We can appreciate the differences in our students and provide learning experiences which allow them to develop their full potential.

I urge teachers to acknowledge their Personality Factor, have the courage to be themselves and appreciate the differences in those students in their care.

Chapter Four
The Personality Factor and Mental Health

THERE SEEMS TO HAVE been a documented increase of poor mental health problems over the past ten years or so. Is this because the issue of mental health is now more out in the open or are we failing to provide adequate support amidst the ever-changing world we live in? Are we still doing the same things expecting to get different results? The dynamics of the Personality Factor are complex, yet I just want to put this out there. I can't help wondering whether knowing our Personality Factor may contribute positively to our mental well-being. I can only relate my own experiences. Nonetheless there may perhaps be a place for the Personality Factor to be considered in relation to Mental Health.

According to the World Health Organisation,

> *'Mental health is a state of mental well-being that enables people to cope with the stresses of life, realise their abilities, learn well and work well, and contribute to their community. It has intrinsic and instrumental value and is integral to our well-being'.*

The Australian Government states on their website that,

> 'Mental health is a state of wellbeing that enables you to deal with what life throws at you. It is about feeling resilient, enjoying life and being able to connect with others.'

It also states that good mental health helps you:

- *cope with the normal stresses of life*
- *be productive both at work and in your private life*
- *relate well to other people*
- *contribute to your community.*

THE PERSONALITY FACTOR

I can largely attribute my ability to persevere through the many adversities I faced mainly throughout the second half of my life, to learning about my Personality Factor. It helped me know who I am. It allowed me to make sense of my marriage breakup, and it allowed me to support my children as well as I could while they were in my immediate care. Considering my beliefs, I can only hope that I went some way towards providing an accepting environment which allowed them to become the people they are innately meant to be. I am proud of all my children and what they have achieved as adults, given the challenging circumstances they faced while growing up. Without the insights I gained from knowing the Personality Factor, I believe my struggle could have been much tougher.

Even though a little tension may be a good thing, there are a myriad of factors which cause stress in our lives. Stress can occur when our needs and values are not being fulfilled and our talents are not being utilised. Stress may be caused by a lack of basic necessities needed to exist. Anxiety might be produced by not knowing who you are and where you fit in. Conflict in relationships at home and at work is also a component of stress. However, have you ever considered that those things which cause stress for some people may be a source of enjoyment for others. Some may be stressed by having to speak in public while others revel in the opportunity. Some may find that meeting new people is a cause for stress whereas others thrive on that activity. For some, socialising is an essential part of their lifestyle. For others, socialising may be a constant source of distress.

Stress is personal so you are the best one to learn how to handle it. Acknowledging your Personality Factor may help you recognise your own stress triggers, understand how you react to stress and find coping techniques that work for you. The more you understand your Personality Factor, the greater capacity you have to manage your stress levels. This may be key to building resilience and to better cope with stresses which impact your mental health.

Maslow's Hierarchy of Needs and the Personality Factor

I first learned about Maslow's hierarchy of needs in the early 1970's when I started teaching in schools. It is now also widely used in health and social work as a framework for assessing clients' needs.

Maslow expounded a more holistic approach to human growth and development. He claimed that the basic needs necessary for survival must be met before higher-level needs would begin to motivate behaviour. However, some do argue that a person's needs may operate on many levels at the same time. They may be motivated by higher growth needs while at the same time dealing with lower-level deficits.

There are five levels in Maslow's hierarchy of needs. From the bottom upwards, the needs are physiological, safety, love and belonging, esteem and self-actualisation.

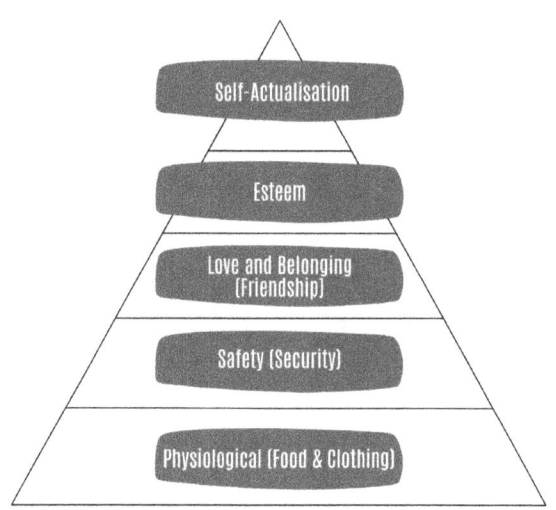

Maslow's Hierarchy of Needs (simplypsychology.org)

To apply Maslow's hierarchy of needs in your life, you start by addressing your basic physiological needs first. Ensure you get adequate sleep, nutrition and exercise. Then focus on safety needs by creating a stable environment. Next, satisfy social needs by building positive relationships for support and belonging. Finally, self-esteem needs are fulfilled by recognising achievements which foster self-confidence.

According to Maslow, the highest-level needs relate to self-actualisation. He maintains it is a process by which we achieve our full potential. He espouses that self-actualising people have both a more efficient perception of reality and more comfortable relations with it. They accept themselves and others.

So how does the Personality Factor fit into this?

A central concept in Carl Jung's analytical psychology is the process of Individuation. It represents the lifelong process of self-realisation and self-understanding. It's about fulfilling your unique potential and becoming the person that you are innately meant to be, seeking to achieve a state of wholeness and harmony.

While the first four levels of Maslow's pyramid could be common to everyone, the fifth level of self-actualisation may not be shared according to the Personality Factor. Different Personality Factors may have different self-actualisation or Individuation needs.

If we are mindful of our Personality Factor, self-actualisation means different things to different people. There are also stressors which affect different temperaments in different ways. The strategies to counteract those stressors are also not the same for each Personality Factor. Not having your self-actualisation needs catered to in the way that Jung suggested may perhaps explain why people who seemingly have their basic needs met, still have poor mental health. Often people have the necessities of physical, security and love needs met, yet they fail to cope with the normal stresses of life. Teenagers who come from a loving and caring family may still have poor mental health issues. This is alarming to parents and teachers who are at a loss to understand what may be causing this.

Self-actualisation for people with **NF** temperaments include authenticity and a search for meaning and significance. They tend to over-stretch themselves and may have difficulty with structure, authority figures and rules. When this happens, they may suffer a loss of integrity or identity. One way to counteract that stress is to have time alone, then seek out others who can provide warmth and empathy.

For people with the **NT** temperament, self-actualisation involves mastery and self-control, along with knowledge and competence. They can be stressed by experiencing incompetence because they realise that they cannot know and do all things well. They always seem to be escalating their standards. Stress may be offset by exploring a concept or having a problem to solve.

Membership and belonging, responsibility and duty are the core needs for the **SJ** temperament to achieve self-actualisation. They may be impatient with complications and can worry about anticipated problems. They are stressed by rejection and exclusion. To lessen their stress, these people need you to let them know they are needed. They want to help and be of service.

When it comes to people with the **SP** temperament, self-actualisation comes by having the freedom to act on impulse and the ability to make an impact. They may be impatient with abstractions and for them, routine can lead to rigidity. Stress may also come from constant constraint or delay. To compensate for these stresses, they need action to restore their equilibrium.

I would also suggest that some of our self-esteem needs (Maslow's fourth level of hierarchy) are similarly linked to our Personality Factor.

People with the **NF** temperament need personal expressions of appreciation to boost their confidence and self-esteem. Constantly having to succumb to impersonal treatment may cause their self-worth to be eroded.

If people with the **NT** temperament are being constantly asked to perform routine tasks, or are asked to do things which violate logic, reason or principle, it may have a damaging effect on their confidence and self-esteem. To boost their self-worth, they need to be appreciated for their capabilities and ideas.

When people with the **SJ** temperament are frequently commended for their loyalty, responsibility, and industriousness, their self-worth will be enhanced. On the other hand, if they are constantly being faced with deadlines not being met and standard operational procedures not being adhered to, then this may cause harmful deterioration of their confidence.

Constantly being told how to work, and persistently being required to adhere to standard operational procedures may have a detrimental effect on the confidence of a person with the **SP** temperament. Having others commend them for their endurance, cleverness, adaptation and timing will contribute to their self-worth.

To simplify this here we can look at the four Temperament Types and self-actualisation.

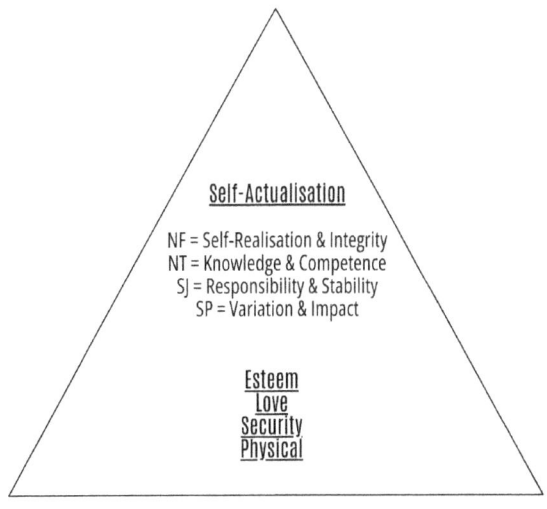

Even though our basic survival needs are met, it is possible that our self-actualisation needs are NOT being met according to our Personality Factor. This could be contributing to poor mental health in some. Despite our best intentions, we are perhaps not differentiating the needs of self-actualisation for everyone. If our self-actualisation needs are being met from the perspective of the Personality Factor, and we are not constantly trying to be something we are not, we have a better capacity to support our wellbeing in a more positive way.

This knowledge about differing self-actualisation and esteem requirements served me well when working with students in high schools. It allowed the students to gain better self-awareness and to take responsibility for managing issues which caused them to come to me in the first place. The students were referred to me by teachers for poor behaviour or low academic achievement, and some self-referred. Many of the students were grappling with issues including low self-esteem, conflict with parents, teachers and peers, and bullying. I observed that most seemed to know who they are but had trouble reconciling that knowledge with the world around them. Many had trouble fitting in and seemed to be at odds with differing outlooks and expectations of their parents and teachers. Other people seemed different from them, though they couldn't understand why others didn't see things their way.

Teenagers think that they are right, and they often are – for them. When they are in this stage of their development, it may be difficult for them to see that other people with a differing Personality Factor may be right too. It was easy for me to see that many of the clashes between teenagers and parents, and teenagers and teachers are inevitable among individuals with different Personality Factors. I helped them see that while they can't change other people, they could change the way they reacted to different situations.

I used my knowledge of the Personality Factor to encourage students to become more resilient in their style. Knowledge of their Personality Factor helped them to take responsibility for how they handled various situations they found themselves in. It helped them devise strategies to manage those situations, allowing them to better cope with the stresses of being a teenager. Students also reported that it helped them to relate to other people more easily. Most of all it helped the students gain a better understanding of who they are.

I believe there is significant merit in taking different approaches when supporting people to achieve confidence and self-actualisation. I didn't truly start to know myself until my mid-thirties. I grew up in a family who didn't allow me to blossom in the manner that my natural disposition would have enjoyed, so I dutifully adhered to the expectations of my family, my school and society in general. I had spent almost half a lifetime trying to be someone I was not, in order to fit in. I mastered the art of looking like I'm okay, and I have had my fair share of poor mental health issues. Even now, I sometimes still don't feel confident in my abilities. But applying the Personality Factor in my life has certainly assisted with my process. Knowing my own stressors and how to counteract them has allowed me to better cope with the normal stresses of my life.

It has also helped me to choose the right therapist to assist me in my journey. There are many excellent types of therapies available. However, some were more suited to me than others. Often people will accept the first helping professional they go to. Some will feel adequately catered for while others will be more confused than ever or seemingly get poor results. Knowing your Personality Factor can assist you to become more discerning about the helpers you access. It allows you to move on to find a more suitable provider.

I recall one time I had an experience with a counsellor who was not meeting my needs. With my new knowledge and understanding of myself, I was able to find someone more suitable. In the first session, I was asked if I had been in counselling before and what had worked best. I explained that I prefer a more humanistic approach. In the next session, the counsellor proceeded to take a behaviouralist approach and practically lectured me on what I should do. She gave me material to read that I was already familiar with and didn't once ask me to explain what was going on for me when I explained I was feeling stressed and anxious. This approach did little for my waning self-confidence and self-esteem. If helpers had a better understanding of the Personality Factor, they may see that their favoured approach may not be suitable for everyone. It would allow them to refer a client to someone else or enable them to modify their approach more flexibly.

Bullying and the Personality Factor

The World Health Organisation cites bullying as a leading risk factor for mental health conditions. The worrying thing for me is that bullying doesn't seem to abate despite the increased efforts to educate people. Some people may become bullies because it is a learned coping strategy. Others might choose to bully because they are bored, while others may merely think it is a cool thing to do. When I was working in schools, I ran anti-bullying classes. Various organisations were also invited to run sessions about bullying using music and drama. The students keenly participated in the activities and were quizzed about what they had learned. In all cases, the students were generally very knowledgeable in the understanding of what bullying is and what they could do to reduce it. However, nothing changed. The students who eagerly participated in the sessions were the same students who continued bullying practices. Those students who had allowed themselves to be bullied, continued to be bullied. I felt powerless to curb the incidence of bullying on my watch. Believing I have also been a victim of bullying in many of my workplaces, I often felt powerless, at times, to handle situations I regularly found myself in.

I began to wonder whether some forms of bullying may be related to the Personality Factor. Is there a connection between how bullying is perceived by adversaries with differing Personality Factors? The behaviour which is deemed as bullying to some may not have been seen as bullying to others. I wondered whether some forms of bullying are in the eye of the perceiver.

In my workplaces, I have regularly clashed with management. My treatment by management had all the hallmarks of bullying. Maybe it was, or was it a clash of Personality Factors? Upon reflection, while I'm not excusing many of the behaviours, there was a distinct mismatch of Personality Factors between me and the offending managers. I couldn't see things in black and white and I thought I was being personally attacked. In hindsight, I realise that may not have entirely been the case. The same behaviour from the manager may not have been seen as an attack by someone who was more practical and logical in their approach. Nevertheless, these interactions constantly caused me significant amounts of stress and anxiety. Even with my knowledge of the Personality Factor, I sometimes found it difficult to negotiate my workplace environment effectively. It appeared that the managers had no knowledge of the Personality Factor and did not think for one moment that their behaviour might be seen as bullying by some. I had some colleagues who supported me in my claims. However, most of my allegations were dismissed. It has been my experience that many people in my workplaces accepted those actions by staff and very few reported perceived bullying from managers.

Quite likely those who do the most bullying are those who don't see anything wrong with their behaviours. So, I question whether we are looking at preventing bullying in the correct way. It may be difficult to curb the behaviour that could be perceived as bullying when many bullies do not seem to accept that they are, in fact, bullying. Non-threatening education using the Personality Factor may benefit both the bully and the victim. Both parties could know themselves better and have an understanding that other people may not see things the way they do.

Surely much of the responsibility lies with the perceived victim. I know that, for myself, I was better able to deal with the situation when I managed my reactions more effectively. I remembered that I couldn't change other people. I could only regulate my own response to their behaviours. It may be important to increase confidence and self-esteem in those who feel they are bullied, particularly with children and teenagers. It may be more important to provide differing approaches to help the perceived victim of bullying to better manage their reactions. Remember, sustaining resilience is different for different people. If we are mindful of our Personality Factor, we may have a better understanding of why the perceived victim feels bullied. If we are in a helping role, we can suggest strategies pertinent to everyone individually to strengthen their confidence and resilience.

As for the bullies, perhaps we can approach curbing their behaviours in a different way. In schools especially, rather than punishing the bullies, a restorative approach may be more appropriate. If the fundamental cause of bullying behaviour comes from boredom or learned coping strategies, then surely focusing on the underlying cause rather than the behaviour is necessary. Allowing bullies to be useful and help in a school project or assist teachers with classroom preparation or the like, could be beneficial for all concerned. It may result in raising the self-esteem and confidence of the bully to a point where the bullying behaviour is no longer required to mask the issue of boredom or coping.

Mental health

The Australian Government states on their website that 'good mental health allows you to be productive both at work and in your private life'. Maybe it's the other way round. When you know yourself and are productive at work and in your private life, then maybe good mental health will follow. If you are using your natural talents, then your path through life is likely to take less effort, increase effectiveness, and produce better results.

We are able to learn many skills and we must do so during our lifetime. However, some of the skills we must learn come more easily and naturally to us than others. When we are constantly having to use learned skills that don't come naturally to us far more than those which align with our Personality Factor, we run the risk of becoming more stressed than is acceptable. This in turn might lead to both poor physical health and poor mental health. The knowledge of my Personality Factor helped me understand where my strengths and talents lie. I discovered what might cause me stress in both my work and private lives. I was also able to discover techniques for managing that stress.

The Personality Factor is a valuable, non-threatening approach to use to reach and sustain positive mental health. I urge you to take up the challenge to investigate more fully the impact that knowing your Personality Factor may have on your wellbeing in your pursuit of maintaining resilience, productivity, relationships and community connections.

Conclusion

EVERYONE IS AN INDIVIDUAL with his or her own life history, and clearly there is much more to people than purely their Personality Factor. The Personality Factor is simply a part of the larger lifelong endeavour of getting to know who we are. We have our own idiosyncrasies and experiences. We are like some other people and yet like no one else.

Life is never as straightforward as simply knowing the Personality Factor. Nonetheless, even a little understanding may help, and I am truly grateful for the insights I have gained through knowing my own Personality Factor. Therefore, I urge everyone including parents, teachers and helpers to look at your own Personality Factor. Are you considering the Personality Factor of those you are working with or helping, or are you merely supporting them in a way that typically suits you and others with the same Personality Factor as you?

I believe that exploring the Personality Factor is not just for corporate businesses to enhance their operations and provide insights for their workers to excel in their organisations. It is also for the everyday person who wants to be the best they can be. It is for people who want to change the way they do things to get better results than they may have hoped for.

We all know the adage 'Knowledge is Power' – use it but don't abuse it. Effective use of the Personality Factor has the potential to enrich your life and that of others. However, it is important to use your newfound knowledge wisely.

Use it to:

- Understand yourself better.

- Make effective use of your natural strengths and minimise your challenges.

- Better understand others and communicate more fruitfully with them.

Remember, not everyone likes or knows about the Personality Factor. It is important to be sensitive to other people and not use it to stereotype, attack or limit them. Use the Personality Factor to know yourself but not to excuse your own performance or behaviour, and please be cautious about guessing someone else's Personality Factor and assuming that your conclusion is correct.

Also remember that just because you know and understand the Personality Factor, it does not mean you believe in the differences. I have come across many who say they see how others are different, but then proceed to expect or want those people to be more like them and do things the same way as they would. There is a vast leap between knowing the differences and accepting and celebrating those differences. What is that saying? You'll see it when you believe it.

I wish that this belief in the Personality Factor may help:

- Bridge the communication gap in relationships in our work and personal life and between parents and children – especially teenagers.

- Give an awareness to better handle life's stresses to maintain good mental health.

- Provide a framework to allow us to take responsibility for how we manage situations in a way that contributes positively to our wellbeing.

Most of all I wish that we know ourselves. Learning about the Personality Factor is a great way to know yourself without being accusative. The more we know ourselves, the more able we are to take responsibility for maintaining good relationships with ourselves and others. This also gives us the capacity to better cope with many of the adversities we may encounter.

Give yourself permission to be yourself and appreciate and celebrate the differences in other people.

I have provided a comprehensive list of resources at the end of this book. However, here is a quick guide to current resources for finding out more about the Personality Factor based on Carl Jung's works on psychological types.

For general information:

- http://www.myersbriggs.org/
- https://www.itd.net.au/
- http://keirsey.com

For MBTI® Accreditation:

- www.themyersbriggs.com

For Parents, Teachers, and Children:

- https://elizabethmurphymmtic.com/
- www.peoplestripes.org
- www.personalitypuzzles.com

- https://www.itd.net.au/

For MMTIC® Accreditation:

- www.peoplestripes.org

Useful Resources

Websites:

- http://www.myersbriggs.org/
- www.themyersbriggs.com
- www.peoplestripes.org
- https://elizabethmurphymmtic.com/
- www.personalitypuzzles.com
- https://www.itd.net.au/
- https://lindaberens.com/
- http://keirsey.com
- www.ausapt.org.au

- The Evil Practice of Narcotherapy. – The Blog of David Mark Keirsey (wordpress.com)

- Maslow's Hierarchy of Needs (simplypsychology.org

- https://www.who.int/news-room/fact-sheets/detail/mental-health-strengthening-our-response

- https://www.health.gov.au/topics/mental-health-and-suicide-prevention/about-mental-health#:~:text=Mental%20health%20is%20a%20state,the%20normal%20stresses%20of%20life

- https://www.google.com.au/books/edition/Walden/FAE-Ou4lPbwC?hl=en&gbpv=1&printsec=frontcover

Books:

PLEASE UNDERSTAND ME II: Temperament, Character, Intelligence
by David Keirsey (Author)
Publisher: Prometheus Nemesis Book Co; First Edition (January 1, 1998)
ISBN 1-885705-02-6

The Developing Child: Using Jungian Type to Understand Children

by Elizabeth Murphy (Author)
Publisher: UNKNO; First Edition (January 19, 1992)
ISBN-0-89106-060-X

Differentiated Coaching: A Framework for Helping Educators Change Second Edition
by Jane A. G. Kise (Author)
Publisher: Corwin; Second edition (June 21, 2017)
ISBN-13: 978-1506327754

Differentiation Through Personality Types: A Framework for Instruction, Assessment, and Classroom Management 1st Edition
by Jane A. G. Kise (Author)
Publisher: Corwin; 1st edition (December 12, 2006)
ISBN-13: 978-1412917704

Discovering Type with Teens
by Mollie Allen (Author), Claire Hayman(Author), Kay Abella (Author), Eleanor Sommer (Editor)
Publisher: Center for Applications of Psychological Type, Inc. (March 23, 2010)
ISBN-13: 978-0935652895

The Chemistry of Personality: A Guide to Teacher-Student Interaction in the Classroom
by Elizabeth Murphy (Author), Eleanor Sommer (Editor)
Publisher: Center for Applications of Psychological Type; 1st

edition (July 18, 2008)
ISBN-10: 0935652825

MMTIC® Manual by Elizabeth Murphy and Charles Meisgeier (CAPT 2008)
by Elizabeth Murphy (Author), Charles Meisgeier (Author)
ISBN-13: 978-0935652819

Looking at Type and Learning Styles
by Gordon D. Lawrence (Author)
Publisher: Center for Applications of Psychological Type (January 1, 1997)
ISBN-13: 978-0935652338

People Types and Tiger Stripes: Using Psychological Type to Help Students Discover Their Unique Potential
by Gordon D. Lawrence (Author), Eleanor Sommer (Editor)
Publisher: Center for Applications of Psychological Type; 4th edition (September 7, 2009)
ISBN-13: 978-0935652871

Type Talk: The 16 Personality Types That Determine How We Live, Love and Work: 16 Personality Types That Determine How We Live, Love, Work
by Kroeger, Otto, Thuesen, Janet M.
published by Bantam Doubleday Dell Publishing Group (1988)
ISBN: 0-385-29828-5

Applications of the Myers Briggs Type Indicator in Higher Education
by Judith Provost (Author), Anchors Scott (Author)
Publisher: Center for Applications of Type (January 1, 1987)
ISBN-13: 978-0891060321

Effective Teaching, Effective Learning: Making the Personality Connection in Your Classroom 1st Edition (October 18, 1995) by Alice M. Fairhurst (Author), Lisa L. Fairhurst (Author)
Format: Kindle Edition
ISBN 0-89106-078-2
Publisher: Nicholas Brealey

My Personality
by Mary McGuiness
IBSN 0 9851888 3 6
Published by. Mary Mac Books. June 2007.

You've Got Personality: An Introduction to the Personality Types described by Carl Jung and Isabel Myers
by Mary McGuiness
ISBN 0 975888 0 1
Published by. Mary Mac Books. 2004

Gifts Differing: Understanding Personality Type
by Isabel Briggs Myers (Author), Peter B. Myers (Author)

Publisher: CPP; (January 1, 1995)
ISBN-13: 978-0891060741

Families: Using Type to Enhance Mutual Understanding
by Charles W Ginn (Author), Charles W. Ginn (Author)
Publisher: Center for Applications of Psychological Type (January 1, 1995)
ISBN-13: 978-0935652260

Looking at Type and Learning Styles
by Gordon D. Lawrence (Author)
Publisher: Center for Applications of Psychological Type (January 1, 1997)
ISBN-: 978-0935652338

The M.O.M.S. Handbook
by Janet P. Penley (Author)
Publisher: Penley & Associates, Incorporated; (January 1, 1999)
ISBN-13: 978-0965697409

Introduction to Type
by Isabel Briggs Myers
Published by CPP 2015
ISBN-13: 978-1856390675

Introduction to Type Dynamics
by Linda K. Kirby (Author)

Publisher: CPP (January 1, 2000)
ISBN-13: 978-1856390774

The Undiscovered Self: The Dilemma of the Individual in Modern Society
by Carl G Jung (Author)
Publisher: Berkley Books (7 February 2006)
ISBN-13: 978-0451217325

Walden: The Original 1854 Edition (A Henry David Thoreau Classics)
Publisher: Independently published (1 February 2023)
ISBN-13: 979-8374732030

About the Author

Dianne Langley

Dianne is a Certified Myers-Briggs Type Indicator (MBTI®) Practitioner and has been involved in education and in the co-ordination of programs for children, teenagers, and adults for most of her working life.

She has taught in Primary and Secondary Schools, and in TAFE Colleges. She has also worked for various Government agencies and private training providers where she has conducted career planning and personal development programs, staff training and counselling.

www.ingramcontent.com/pod-product-compliance
Lightning Source LLC
Chambersburg PA
CBHW052053070526
44584CB00017B/2166